The Kitchen in History

The Kitchen in History

Molly Harrison

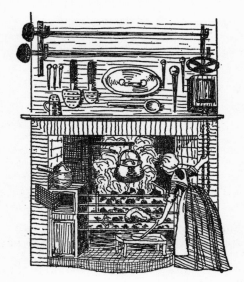

CHARLES SCRIBNER'S SONS
NEW YORK

The drawings in the text are by Sheila Maguire

The following photographs are from the magazine archives of *Caterer &
Hotel Keeper*, to whom the author and publishers wish to express their
thanks: 50, 51, 52, 53, 54, 57, 58, 59, 60, 61, 63, 64, 65, 66, 67 and 68

For Georgina, who is an imaginative
but somewhat violent cook and likes to have
her mother as kitchen-maid

Contents

Photographs

Drawings in the text

Prehistoric times
1 Bronze ladle, fifth century BC
2 Bronze hanging pots, third century BC

Roman Britain
3 Chopper blade, flesh-hooks, kitchen scissors and
   a skewer
4 Tripod bowl, mortar and sieve

The Anglo-Saxons
5 Cooking
6 Drinking-horn and silver spoon

The Middle Ages
7 Cup dogs and basket spit
8 Brass curfews
9 Earthenware pots and iron skillet
10 Chimney cranes and pot-hangers
11 Idleback and kettle
12 Frying-pan and girdlepan on pot-hooks
13 Iron trivets
14 Medieval feasting
15 Sugar loaf and cutters
16 Spinning and carding wool
17 Lanterns of horn and metal
18 A medieval vineyard

The sixteenth century
19 Mortar and pestle, nutmeg grater and spice box
20 Hour-glass
21 Preparing for a feast
22 Earthenware pitcher, horn mug and pewter mug
23 Spiral iron candlesticks

Our English housewife must be of chaste thought, stout courage, patient, untired, watchful, diligent, witty, pleasant, constant in friendship, full of good neighbourhood, wise in discourse, but not frequent therein . . . comfortable in her counsels, and generally skilful in all the worthy knowledge which do belong to her vocation.

Gervase Markham: *English Hus-wife* (1616)

I

Evidence and Perspective

HUMAN affairs are always changing, yet there are periods when mankind seems to stand still and others when he rushes forward at an alarming rate. Since everything in history is interconnected, the small with the infinitely great, such changes of tempo and emphasis spread inevitably beyond public and general affairs into the life of the individual and the family.

Homes have, however, always tended to change less than other social institutions and until very recent times the kitchen and all its works have changed even less than other parts of the house. From primitive fire to modern cooker has been a long, slow process. We are all conservative in our daily habits and a housewife who runs a home smoothly and happily, runs it along accepted, routine lines.

The kitchen is the working centre of the home, the most used room in the house, so it can justifiably claim to be the most important. Perhaps its claim to historical influence is greater even than that of the bedroom. Man certainly cannot live by bread alone, but neither can he live without it, or its equivalent.

This book is not concerned with the kitchen just as a room, but rather as a centre of influence. That influence, of course, predated the construction of any separate room: housewives existed before houses, cooks before cookers and clothes were made and laundered centuries before man had invented, for women's use, the spinning wheel or the sewing machine, the tap or the detergent. The basic processes, indeed, have not changed at all—boiling, baking, scrubbing and much else happen now almost exactly as they have done from earliest times.

How do we know about the kitchens, dairies, laundries, pantries and sewing rooms of our ancestors? What they contained, how they were used, and who worked there? Hearsay is always a poor guide and history books tend to ignore such mundane, everyday matters. Great events do not usually happen in kitchens.

Letters and diaries, wills and inventories sometimes give us sketchy evidence, though inevitably this is usually related to wealthy families living in grand houses. The ordinary man or woman could rarely write, had little spare time in which to do so if he could, and anyway had little to write about and few belongings to bequeath at the end.

Pictorial evidence is more vivid and real than any writing, but paintings or drawings of kitchen life are few and far between. This is not surprising when we remember that patrons have normally employed artists to record success, achievement and the grander moments of life. The art of homely observation has only occasionally and at certain periods been appreciated. The housewife and her servants have always created both warp and weft of the fabric of home life, but we catch only rare glimpses of them as they have gone busily about their duties through the centuries.

The real, the most solid evidence we have of the day-to-day work of the kitchen lies in the actual utensils and equipment which have survived and which we can see and sometimes handle in museums, historic houses and antique shops. We may have to guess at the exact ways in which some of them were used, but there can be no doubt that most served their purpose well and so have not much changed their design in many centuries.

Housekeeping is now far simpler than it has ever been before. There is less to do now that crèches, schools, hospitals, laundries, dry-cleaners, restaurants, factories and supermarkets have taken over much of the work previously done at home. Many social regulations—about smokeless zones, pedestrian precincts, food and drug analysis and weights and measures inspection, for example—give communal support to every housewife's responsibilities. And innumerable pieces of electrical equipment are time- and labour-saving to a degree which would have seemed magical even a century ago. The kitchen fire is no longer the heart or the focal point of most homes; where it has not yet been usurped by central heating systems, its place has been taken by the television screen and the picture window. There is loss and gain on both sides of the equation, none of us can know the future, or accurately assess the past.

Social history is inevitably pieced together as a mosaic, and this story of the kitchen particularly so. If it seems at some times a repetitive story, at others perhaps a somewhat contradictory one, the fault lies in ourselves—in those multitudes of housewives who, by habit or by improvisation, have worked and planned, laughed and cried and struggled, to feed, clothe and bring up husbands and children, look after pets and entertain guests. We have not created a tidy story or a very logical one, but we know in our hearts that it has always been important.

Thomas Tusser, the agricultural writer and poet who farmed at Cattawade in Suffolk and introduced the culture of barley, knew this

well. In 1557 in 'Book of Huswiferie' – one of the many sections in his
A hundreth good pointes of husbandrie – put it charmingly:

Take weapon away, of what force is a man?
Take huswife from husband and what is he then?

Though husbandry seemeth to bring in the gains
Yet huswifery labours seem equall in pains

Some respit to husbands the wether may send
But huswives affairs have never an end.

2

Prehistoric Times

I T was in the desert oases and river valleys of the Tigris, the Euphrates and the Nile that men first tamed animals and began to breed them for food. Here, too, where the climate gave easier conditions of living and where the soil was so rich that wild plants produced their crops two or three times in a single year, the idea developed of deliberately sowing seeds and harvesting. We do not know which plants were the first to be cultivated, but the cereal grasses certainly came to be the most important and, once regular food was available, a more settled way of life became possible. Women could keep a store of grain and dried meat and fish and plan their families' meals; herding animals is less time-consuming and less tiring than hunting them, so there was time and energy for thinking and inventing. The result was the gradual development of the crafts of pottery, weaving, basketry and metal-working.

The introduction of pottery was of course a great step forward:

Not only does it provide the housewife with more convenient vessels, much more easily manufactured than the stone bowls laboriously carved and ground out of solid blocks, but it represents a very important technological stage. Man, instead of simply fashioning an artifact out of natural material, has discovered that he can alter some of these materials. By making a mixture of clay, grit and straw and subjecting it to high temperature, he has actually altered the nature of his material and given it new properties. This is the beginning of a very important industrial revolution . . . concerning the origins of which we still know very little. We do not know yet whether the idea, at least, if not the full process, spread from one centre, or if it was evolved in a number of places independently.

The author of those words, Kathleen Kenyon, worked for many years as director of excavations at Jericho, a few miles from the River Jordan. Jericho is the earliest town to have been discovered and excavated, and was a flourishing community at a time when, in other areas, men were nomadic hunters. Many successive Jerichos have been unearthed on the site; the earliest of them dates from about 7000 BC.

Many of the houses of early Jericho were large, and the rooms were grouped round courtyards which were used for cooking. Several layers of hearths have been found there, built one on top of the other, with innumerable layers of ashes separated by thin clay floors. It seems likely that when a floor became dirty from the ashes and greasy from the cooking, a new one was laid. The clay floors were covered with a very fine plaster, often coloured red or cream and highly polished, so we know that the women were house-proud even then.

Under these houses were others, much earlier, and beehive-shaped; timber was extensively used, for remains of burnt beams have been unearthed. Dishes and bowls of stone have been found; no doubt other containers were of wood or skin but have not survived. Dr Kenyon tells us:

> Their tools and weapons were mainly of flint . . . there
> are many varieties and sizes of blades, which served as
> knives. There are borers and scrapers which would serve
> for manufacturing garments and containers of skin.
> Arrowheads showed that hunting still supplemented
> food production. . . .

Evidence that these people used grain comes from the frequent finding of querns—roughly oblong blocks of stone used for grinding corn. There is a grinding hollow into which the grain was put, and at the end of the stone a flat ledge on which perhaps the operator sat. A great many oval grinding stones have been found in Jericho, and also polishing stones, shaped like cakes of soap with two convex surfaces polished to an almost mirror-like finish. The larger stones were probably used for burnishing the plastered floors, and the smaller ones for polishing the stone bowls and tools.

In colder northern climates development was inevitably slower and towns for a long time unknown. In Britain men were living in groups of huts on downs and by lakesides by about 3000 BC. They had learnt how to build huts with timber supports and had provided themselves with a cooking-place—a rough floor of baked clay, with layers of stone dividing it from the rest of the dwelling. On Dartmoor, near Buckfast Abbey, there are the remains of a settlement of small huts, each with a sheltering wall to screen the doorway from the prevailing west wind. The floor was of beaten clay, the roof probably of branches covered with turf, and drainage was provided by siting the huts on sloping ground. At the highest part of the interior, on the right of the entrance, was a low stone dais or bench which, covered with fern or heather, would have been used as a seat by day and a bed by night.

In these huts there are stone-lined cooking pits near the centre roof-poles. There is in many cases a heap of fire-cracked pebbles by each pit, and from one hearth in a hut at Hay Tor two barrow-loads of charcoal have been removed. At another hut nearby a round-based pot was found actually in position in one of the stone-lined cooking holes, and inside it was a fire-cracked flint. Both had lain there, covered in earth, for over 4,000 years!

At Skara Brae in the Orkney Isles there still stand, huddled together, a dozen little houses and a workshop which were built around 1500 BC. There were no trees on the windswept isles, so the settlers used local stone to build their walls, their roofs and their furniture, and fortunately this stone does not perish. The roofs have long since fallen in, but we can still see that each house had one almost circular living room and one or more little side alcoves which were probably used as storehouses and privies. There was a peat fire in the middle of the earthen floor and the smoke drifted out through a hole in the roof. A box bed of stone and a kind of stone dresser stood against the walls.

At Jarlshof in Shetland are ruins of Bronze and Iron Age settlements, from which we know that their inhabitants built small 'wheelhouses' within enclosing dry-stone walls. Each wheel-house had curved walls forming a little room opening on to a central hearth; it was roofed with stone slabs and sealed against the weather with turves, leaving a central hole above the hearth. There were no windows and light was provided from small stone lamps, which have been found. These settlements were gradually abandoned because the sand, blown by the constant high winds from the Atlantic, was continually piling up over them.

1 Bronze ladle, fifth century BC

The inhabitants must often have had to dig their way in and out in terror, before they finally fled.

The early Iron Age lake villages at Glastonbury and Meare in Somerset have also been explored in detail. There is a hearth of baked clay near the centre of each hut; these must have been frequently replaced, for in one hut thirteen hearths were found, one upon the other. Cone-shaped clay ovens were found at Meare, and at Glastonbury a number of small cakes were discovered, made of unground wheat grains which had been mixed, probably with honey, and baked.

A primitive way of cooking, observed by Charles Darwin, the naturalist, when he visited Tahiti in the late nineteenth century, gives us an insight into the habits of early man:

> Having made a small fire of sticks, they placed a score of
> stones of about the size of cricket balls on the burning wood.
> In about ten minutes the sticks were consumed and the stone
> hot. They had previously folded up, in small parcels of leaves,
> pieces of beef, fish, ripe and unripe bananas and the tops of
> wild arum. These green parcels were laid in a layer between
> two layers of hot stones and the whole then covered up with
> earth, so that no smoke or steam could escape. In about a
> quarter of an hour the whole was most deliciously cooked.

The climate in Tahiti is clement, and cooking out of doors would always be practical, but in prehistoric huts in colder parts of the world life was less pleasant. A hole in the roof was probably a very ineffective means of drawing off the smoke; a home was a cold, damp and dark place where animals and humans lived together, their areas perhaps separated by some kind of low wall or partition.

2 *Bronze hanging pots, third century BC*

Yet these early people were good craftsmen who could smelt the iron they dug out of rocks and forge it into swords and sickles and knives. They could weave and turn wood and make pots; wheat, barley and oats were grown and many querns and millstones have been found. Their handmills consisted of two flat round stones, one above the other,

7

each with a hole in the centre. Grain was poured into the centre hole and the upper stone was turned by means of an upright handle fixed near its rim. The flour worked its way out between the two stones and was probably caught on a mat on which the mill stood. Primitive grain-grinding devices of this kind are still used in many parts of the world. For example, a grinding stone resembling a rolling-pin is used among American Indians.

At Glastonbury there were expert coopers who knew how to build tubs with wooden staves and hoops; probably the women used these for storing food or for washing. Otherwise such laundry as was done was carried to a nearby stream.

From the knowledge that archeologists have pieced together we know that life in those early homes was hard, and comfort unknown. We have no actual written evidence to depend upon for our understanding of early times in Britain until 300 BC, when Pytheas of Marseilles, a contemporary of Alexander the Great, made a courageous voyage up the west coast of Europe to Britain, Jutland and the Orkney and Shetland Islands. He wrote a description of his voyage, but that has been lost. It was read and used by Strabo, the author of an important historical geography of the Roman Empire. He tells us that Pytheas reported that the climate in Britain was foggy and damp and the people raised quantities of corn. These were the men and women whom the Romans found when their legions landed in Britain in 55 BC.

3

Roman Britain

*F*OR nearly four hundred years Britain formed part of an empire which stretched from Babylon, on the River Euphrates, round both north and south shores of the Mediterranean, up through France and as far north as Hadrian's Wall in Northumberland. The primitive tribes who inhabited this island were quite suddenly in close contact with the best that the older European civilization had achieved in science, in art, in law and in domestic comfort and convenience.

It must have been an extraordinary experience for the early Britons, accustomed to living in haphazard groups of simple huts, to see Roman surveyors at work, setting out the regular chequer-board patterns for streets and squares in the new towns, and to hear talk of baths, of heating rooms by warm-air circulation, and of mosaic floors. Between themselves the natives talked the Celtic language, but Latin had become the universal language throughout the whole empire and had to be understood and spoken by anyone who worked for or with the invaders.

The daily lives of most Britons were of course for a long time little affected by Roman building techniques or by the invaders' superior material comforts. They went on living in isolated farmsteads as they had done for several hundred years before the Roman invasion. They have left few traces of themselves by comparison with the richer families; they lived in small round wooden houses of very simple construction, with home-made furniture and very little in the way of shop-bought possessions. The majority of Britons could not afford mosaic pavements, jewellery or fine pottery.

The Roman house in Italy was built round a small courtyard to exclude the sun, but in Britain the same design was opened up to make the most of what sunshine there was, for warmth and light. A villa was essentially a farmstead, planned for comfort and convenience. Over five hundred of them have been found; they were built of stone, some little better than farm cottages with many outbuildings, others with enormous establishments of a hundred people, such as Fishbourne. Few of the houses of better-off Roman families seem to have had upper stories, but most had at least ten rooms, connected by corridors, so that there was no need to go through one room to get to another.

A sizeable house would have separate rooms for different purposes—a dining-room, a kitchen and bedrooms, and smaller rooms, away from the rest, for the slaves. The dining-room floor was inlaid with mosaic over a concrete base. The plastered walls were painted in bright colours, the wooden furniture elaborate and elegant. The kitchen was next to the *triclinium,* or dining-room, where the diners reclined full length, supported on one elbow, on low couches, and ate with the other hand from a low table, rather than sitting up in a chair. These couches were not used as beds; Romans usually slept on the floor or on a raised stone platform, with mattresses, pillows and blankets.

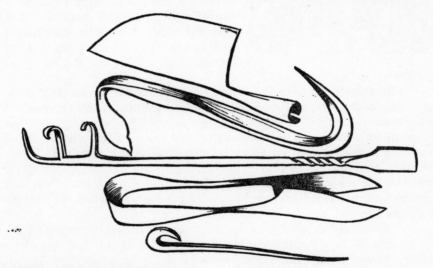

3 Chopper blade, flesh-hooks, kitchen scissors and a skewer

Many of the rooms were heated by a hypocaust, the usual Roman central heating system. A stokehole on an outside wall fed a furnace with charcoal, from which heat spread in channels under the floors and up the walls of the rooms. Even middle-class families had two or three house slaves, who would do the cooking and cleaning, and stoke the furnaces, and the work was divided between the *ordinarii,* who superintended the cleaning, *cellarii*, who looked after the wine, *promi*, who issued daily supplies, *ostarii*, who were door-keepers, *cubicularii*, who cared for the master and introduced his visitors, *coqui*, who were cooks, and *lecticarii*, who carried the litters.

All cooking was done on a charcoal fire on a raised stone hearth. One of these fireplaces was found intact at Pompeii, with a pot still in place, just as it was when Vesuvius erupted and disaster struck the city in the year 79. Pots and pans stood on gridirons over small holes in the top of the stove, and charred food was still in some of the bowls.

The excavations at Pompeii brought to light counterparts of most of the cooking vessels we use today. There were kettles, which hung over the fire, and a *thermospodium*—a kind of hotplate or portable stove on top of which stood pots and dishes to keep food hot until carried into the dining-room. Tripods were used for hanging vessels over the fire and there were funnels, sieves, ladles, knives, spoons and mortars. Some of the spoons had a point at the end, probably for extracting the flesh of shellfish.

4 Tripod bowl, mortar and sieve

In the Via degli Augustali in Pompeii we can still see the so-called 'Forno di Modesto', the oven of the baker Modestus, and we can assume that throughout the Empire similar ovens had been introduced. Only a few minutes before the eruption overwhelmed Pompeii, the baker Modestus had placed eighty-one loaves in the oven, and they were still there, blackened masses of coal, when the iron door of the oven was opened during the excavations nearly 2,000 years later.

In well-to-do Romano-British houses all the kitchen work was done by slaves and it was the task of the lady of the house to supervise them and, presumably, to plan the menus. The following housekeeping account of the year 1 seems curiously lacking in protein foods:

		drachmas	obols
Jan. 16th	Turnips for preserving	1	
	Salt		1
	Grinding 1 artaba of wheat		3
	Rushes for the bread baking		2

		drachmas	obols
Jan. 17th	Pure bread for Prima		$\frac{1}{2}$
Feb. 4th	Lunch for the weaver	1	
	Pure bread for the children		$\frac{1}{2}$
	Beer for the weaver	2	
	Leeks for the weaver's lunch	1	
Feb. 5th	Asparagus for Antas' dinner at the feast of the fuller		$\frac{1}{2}$
	Cabbage for the boys' dinner		$\frac{1}{2}$
Feb. 10th	Savoury		$\frac{1}{2}$
	Rushes for the loaves		$2\frac{1}{2}$
Feb. 11th	Milk for the children		$\frac{1}{2}$
	Barley gruel for the children		$\frac{1}{2}$
Feb. 14th	Sauce	1	
	Pure bread		$\frac{1}{2}$
Feb. 15th	Pomegranates for the children	1	
	Beer	3	
Feb. 18th	2 measures of salt for pickling	2	
	Salt	1	
	Pure bread for the children		$\frac{1}{2}$
	To Secundus for a cake for the children		$\frac{1}{2}$
	Dry finest flour		$\frac{1}{2}$

The Romanized Britons began the day early—often before dawn—with a light breakfast of bread and fruit. A similarly light lunch was taken at midday, at which they ate fish, eggs and vegetables, and drank wine and water. Native beer was drunk as an alternative, though true Romans disliked this. The Emperor Julian, in the fourth century, disliked it so much that he composed a satirical poem attacking it:

On Wine made from Barley

Who made you and from what?
By the true Bacchus I know you not.
He smells of nectar,
But you smell of goat.

The main meal of the day was dinner, which began late in the afternoon, and was an elaborate affair of several courses. The Roman writer Tacitus, son-in-law of Agricola, the best known Governor of Britain, refers to 'elegant banquets' in British houses.

Most households made their own bread and ground their own corn as well. Wheat, barley, oats and rye were used to make both leavened and unleavened bread. Sometimes the loaves were spiced, sometimes flavoured with cheese. Sugar was unknown, so honey was the universal sweetener. Salt, mustard and vinegar were normally served, but pepper was an expensive luxury.

The Romans in exile in Britain found, of course, that the country did not produce many of the plants that, at home, they had been accustomed to use for food and medicines, so before long supplies of such plants were being brought to Britain, and servants taught how to use them. Grapes were grown in Britain in Roman times. In digging foundations near Gloucester a pile of *marc* was found—a crush of grape skin and seeds from some Roman vintage. Terraced vineyards were tended in that region despite frost, conquering armies and bad summers, until the Middle Ages.

Both candles and oil-lamps were used in the home and had to be maintained by the slaves. Pottery lamps were common and several factories for making them were set up in Britain and in other parts of the Empire. The wicks were of oakum or flax and required constant attention from a slave; and a regular supply of vegetable oil had to be ensured. Vitruvius, who wrote an important book on architecture in about 40 BC, remarked on the dirt which oil-lamps deposited on cornices and hangings, and in Rome a slave was usually detailed to wash down the statues after a lamp-lit party.

In their own homes, Roman slaves and peasants used *lychnicus* lamps, made by setting snail shells in clay, and these must certainly have been in use throughout the Empire. Single-spouted clay lamps have been found at the sites of Roman forts in Britain and one writer recorded that it was not necessary for a provincial governor to find lodgings for any soldier who was so poor that he could afford only a single spout as light, so we know that it was customary for each man to carry his own. Probably visitors also carried their own lamps, unless they were going to a very wealthy household.

The earliest evidence of the use of candles dates from the first century, when Pliny the Younger wrote in a letter of candles made from threads of flax coated with pitch, and we can be sure that some Roman soldiers brought a supply to Britain and perhaps taught local people how to make them. We do not know to what extent candles were used domestically, but in the second century another writer, Apuleius, wrote in his satire *The Golden Ass* of *cerii* made of wax and of *lebacii* made of tallow, and described how 'at a noise in the night the household runs with torches, lamps, tallow candles and wax tapers'.

Much attention was paid to sanitation in better Roman homes and from an early date they used jointed drain-pipes and underground sewers. Roman London had no refuse collection, and everyone shot their rubbish into deep pits dug inside the town. When the pits were full or became insanitary the rubbish was covered with soil or old plaster. In such pits remains of broken bowls, jars and dishes have been found, from which we can reconstruct kitchen utensils; pottery flagons for wine, green glass bottles for oil, bowls and dishes of reddish-brown Samian ware, imported from Gaul, and metal knives and spoons.

The cleaning of dirty clothes was done by fullers, who were important people to the Romans, though presumably the 'smalls' were attended to by slaves and ranked as kitchen work. As the fullers bleached, cleaned and stretched new cloth, they presumably also had the equipment necessary for heavy laundry work. Fuller's earth was used, until soap was invented in Gaul early in the first century. The garments were washed by treading them in a large vat and rinsing them in another. In St Mark's Gospel, ix 3, we read: 'And his raiment became shining, exceeding white as snow, so as no fuller on earth can white them.'

At Lullingstone in Kent the owner of a villa in the second century added a laundry. A rough mound at the back, built of brick, tile and stone, was used for bleaching the linen or hanging it out to air after washing it. A furnace provided hot water for a tank which was used for treading out the dirty clothes, as is done in many a small continental town today. There was a hypocaust and, behind that, a drain.

Personal washing was of immense importance to all Romans, and if the Britons were to adopt the Roman way of life they had to acquire a liking for a daily bath. Public baths in towns were built at the expense of the public authority, the *civitas*, and all were welcome to use them. Prosperous families living out of a town had their own bath suites comprising a *frigidarium,* or cold room, a *tepidarium* which was fairly warm and a *caldarium*, which was hot. These baths needed daily cleaning and maintenance and there had to be a slave always ready to massage and anoint whoever wanted a bath.

We do not know whether slaves were permitted to use their masters' private baths, but Seneca, the philosopher, writing in about 57, gives us a vivid picture of the social life in a public bath:

> I am living near a bath; sounds are heard on all sides. . . . The
> men of more sturdy muscle go through their exercises and swing
> their hands heavily weighted with lead; I hear their groans
> when they strain themselves, or the whistling of laboured
> breath when they breathe out after having held in. If one is
> rather lazy, and merely has himself rubbed with unguents, I
> hear the blows of the hand slapping his shoulders, the sound
> varying according as the massagist strikes with flat or hollow
> palm. . . . Or there is someone in the bath who loves to hear the
> sound of his own voice . . . but the hair-plucker from time to
> time raises his thin shrill voice in order to attract attention,
> and is only still himself when he is forcing cries of pain from
> someone else, from whose armpits he plucks the hairs.

The Romans always had one special place in their house for their household gods, small statues which were believed to take care of the home and the family and slaves. Each day, offerings from the food of the family were made to them and we know that at Chedworth Villa, in Gloucestershire, these gods had their altar in a narrow room next to the kitchen. Cicero, in a speech in 57 BC, said:

> Is there anything more hallowed, is there anything more closely hedged about with every kind of sanctity than the home of each individual citizen? Therein he has his altars, his hearth, his household gods, his private worships, his rites and his ceremonies.

The typical gods of Roman Britain were not worshipped corporately, but in private, singly. Vesta was the spirit of the hearth, the Lares of the house, the Penates of the store cupboard, and Janus of the door. What the Roman wanted was the protection of the gods for the safety of his family and for this he was prepared to pay a price, in the sacrifice of an animal or of the first-fruits of his crops. A lamp was kept burning continually before the altars of the household gods.

The Romans were tolerant in their attitude to religion and allowed each man and each people to worship their own gods. As a result many of the Britons went on for a long time worshipping their ancestral Celtic deities—the spirits of nature; others swore allegiance to the new Roman gods; and, later, yet others began, in the fourth century, to listen to the new teachings of Christianity.

The Roman occupation of Britain lasted for about four hundred years. It is incredible that a civilization so long established could have vanished, leaving little trace of its customs or habits and nothing to show but the decaying roads. The Saxons, Danes and Jutes who came to fill the vacuum left when the Romans were withdrawing, were destructive; they drove people from the towns, razed buildings to the ground, and as the legions marched away southwards they took with them all knowledge of personal washing, of house-warming, and of brick-making, glass-blowing and every domestic sign of a great civilization which had lasted a thousand years.

4

The Anglo-Saxons

*T*HE Anglo-Saxons came to this country as pirates, but gradually settled as industrious farmers. They gave England its name and its language; our place-names still tell the tale of their coming and many of the words we use today to describe our homes are the words they used. Their houses, from the chieftain's hall to the peasant's hut, are described for us in the great Anglo-Saxon poem *Beowulf*. We are told of the 'great mead hall', of the 'lofty house', the wooden walls covered with tapestry, the variegated floor; there is frequent reference to the armour, dresses, jewellery and ornaments of which they were proud, of the 'solid cup, the valuable drinking vessel', 'the dear, or precious drinking cup', but nothing of actual food preparation.

Most people cooked in the open air and the possession of a kitchen was a sign of great social importance and enabled a Saxon to aspire to noble rank. We know that cookery was only a rough necessity and had few refinements for the Anglo-Saxons, for their only words for cook *(coc)* and for kitchen *(cycene)* were both taken from the Latin.

They ate great quantities of bread, milk, butter and cheese. A servant was described as a man's *hlaf-oetan,* or loaf-eater, and a chieftain's wife was a *hlaf-dige,* or distributor of bread. Much of their meat was salted and the place in which the salt meat was kept was the *spic-hus,* or bacon-house. They ate quantities of fish, which they boiled in a *cytel,* or kettle. To this day we speak metaphorically of a 'kettle of fish', though our use of the term to describe a culinary vessel is quite different.

The fire, in early days, was used equally for cooking and for warmth, but this of course involved risk. The seventh-century Saxon Archbishop Theodore decreed:

If a woman place her infant by the hearth, and the man put

water in the cauldron, and it boil over, and the child be scalded to death, the woman must do penance for her negligence, but the man is acquitted of blame.

The fire was virtually a bonfire, in the middle of the single room or hall. Bellows were certainly in common use, for the name *boelig* is Anglo-Saxon, but as the original meaning of the word was 'a bag' it is likely that the early bellows were of a very rough type.

The household collected round their lord at the fire—not at the fire*side*, which term only came later, when fire*places* were at the side of a room—and it was here that the stranger was received. There was, quite literally, 'open house' there, for the doors were never shut against any visitor, as we learn from a beautiful comparison made by one of King Edwin's chieftains:

> The present life of man, O King, seems to me like to the swift flight of a sparrow through the hall where you sit at your meal in winter, with your chiefs and attendants, warmed by a fire made in the middle of the hall, whilst storms of rain or snow prevail without; the sparrow, flying in at one door and immediately out at another, whilst he is visible, is safe from the wintry storm, but after this short space of fair weather, he immediately vanishes out of your sight, into the dark winter from which he has emerged.

6 Anglo-Saxon cooking

Cooking pots hung by the fire from some kind of iron trivet and bar-lip pots have been found at a number of early sites. These had two internal horizontal bars on opposite sides of the pot, level with the rim, to allow ropes or thongs to be attached. When the pot hung over the fire, these handles would not be exposed to the heat.

In *Beowulf* we read of feasting in a king's hall, of the queen's bower, and of sleeping places for women and for servants. There is mention of stables, cowsheds, and storerooms for corn, ale and wood, but not of a kitchen.

Dining in private was considered disgraceful. The family and guests sat at a *bord*—literally a board of wood that was brought out for the occasion, placed upon trestles, and taken away again as soon as the meal was finished. In illuminated manuscripts, wherever dinner scenes are represented, the board is always covered with what is evidently a handsome table-cloth, called a 'bord cloth'; the preparation for dinner was called 'laying the board'. We still use this Anglo-Saxon word when we refer to board and lodging, a boarder, a board-room, a chairman of the board.

We do not know how the tables were arranged for meals, but we do know, from the many domestic objects found in the Saxon burial ground at Sutton Hoo, in Suffolk, that a king's household would possess silver spoons, a set of silver bowls and dishes, drinking-horns, bronze cauldrons of different sizes for cooking, and wooden pails for carrying water.

5 *Drinking-horn and silver spoon*

Each drinking-horn had a wide ornamental silver band round the top and a silver mount at the pointed end. In the Sutton Hoo burial ground these were wrapped in a cloth, presumably to keep them from getting tarnished. From this, it is interesting to speculate whether the Saxons believed that their king would have to fend for himself in the after-life, without benefit of slaves!

Glass vessels were a rare luxury and most were imported. Horns, bottles and cups seem often to have been rounded at the bottom, so we know that wealthy households had plenty of servants to wait at table.

When a lesser man died he was usually given only one drinking vessel in his grave: this might be of wood, bound with bronze, an ordinary earthenware pot, or a glass 'tumbler'—which had no foot and so tumbled if it was set down. Some of the Saxon jars which we can see in museums may have been used, not for drink, but for cooking or storing food.

Anglo-Saxon servants were slaves, who were bought and sold and had no protection in law against their masters and mistresses. It was not unusual for servants to be whipped to death by their mistresses. Some of the descriptions of local miracles give us horrible pictures of the cruel treatment of female slaves, in particular. For quite slight offences they were put in fetters and tortured. A servant-girl in Winchester was set upon by thieves and robbed of her master's clothes as she was taking them to the river to wash. Her master assumed that she had been negligent, beat her severely and put her in fetters.

The personal cruelty of the Anglo-Saxons to their servants is in great contrast to the mildness of the laws laid down. A law of the tenth century took account of the rights of servants and stated that:

> If a woman give her maid a whipping with evil malice, and if death is caused by the whipping and the maid be innocent, the mistress is to fast for seven years. If, however, the maid was at fault, the mistress should fast for three years and should do penance for her sins.

Home was a busy place and the housewife was evidently expected to attend carefully to everything, for we are told in an Anglo-Saxon poem that:

> It beseems a damsel to be at her board; a rambling woman scatters words, she is often charged with faults, a man thinks of her with contempt, oft her cheek smites.

Probably house-cleaning was not much considered, and when food requirements had been attended to, the ladies and their maids were busy with spinning and weaving and with needlework and embroidery. They were so skilful in this that Anglo-Saxon needlework, under the name of English work *(opus Anglicum),* was famous all over Europe.

Countrywomen had to work just as hard as men, labouring in the fields or looking after the poultry, and shearing the sheep, as well as carrying out their duties inside the home. But the Church was insistent that no servile work should be done on Sundays or on Saints' Days. In the year 827 a decree was issued which stated that:

> Women shall not do their textile work, nor cut out clothes, nor stitch them together with the needle, nor card wool, nor beat hemp, nor wash clothes in public, nor shear sheep, so there may be rest on the Lord's day. . . .

5

The Middle Ages

'THE Middle Ages' is the name given, in European countries, to those centuries between about the year 1000, when the Vikings first discovered America, and the year 1500, the dawning of the Renaissance.

Calling this period the Middle Ages is merely a convenience for historians nowadays and for students of history. When history came to be recorded systematically after the invention of printing, the only records available were those of very early, classical times. To the new historians the gap between those early times and their own appeared as 'the middle'.

In the Middle Ages the kitchens of the great establishments, both lay and secular, were vast and important buildings. Life, then, was largely communal and the number of people who had to be provided for was often enormous. The dependants of a large abbey might number eight or nine hundred, and many a nobleman had a household of over three hundred.

The medieval abbeys spared no expense in building and equipping kitchens to fit the needs of the brethren, and of the many guests who were entertained in the course of a year. Gloucester, Durham, Canterbury and Jervaulx Abbeys had kitchens of about forty feet in length; the famous abbot's kitchen at Glastonbury, which can still be seen, was octagonal in shape, with a picturesque lantern in the roof, and had ample room for roasting oxen whole, and for a huge turnspit full of small birds. The many castles had large kitchens, too, but the roasting of oxen and the boiling of whole carcasses of pig often had to be done out of doors.

In April 1206 it was commanded that the king's kitchen at Clarendon should be roofed and shingled, and that two new kitchens should be built, and it was 'particularly directed that each kitchen be provided with a furnace sufficiently large to roast two or three oxen'.

The floors and also the walls of a kitchen, large or small, were usually of stone or brick. Wood was burned in the large open fireplace or 'down-hearth', which was at first in the centre of the hall. A typical central hearth can still be seen at Penshurst in Kent. Timber was plentiful and was used recklessly for almost every purpose. The huge logs

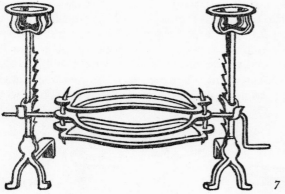

7 Cup dogs and a basket spit

were supported across iron fire-dogs, so named because they resembled dogs in silhouette, the lengthened 'neck' preventing the burning logs from rolling off. Some fire-dogs had small iron cups at their heads, in which vessels would be set to warm drinks. Later, when the fire was moved from its central position, the wall behind the fire was protected by a cast-iron fire-back, which also radiated heat into the room. Both dogs and fire-backs were sometimes ornamented.

It took much time and struggling with sticks and logs, pokers, tongs and bellows, to make and maintain a good fire, so it was the

8 Brass curfews

general custom never to let the kitchen fire go out, but to keep it burning day and night. The kitchen fire was, in fact, the sole source of ignition: Caxton wrote of a man who 'took to his wife an offering-candle and bade her light it at the fire' and in Gerard's *Herball* we read that 'giant puff-balls' were used in some places where neighbours 'dwell farre a sunder, to carrie and reserve fire from place to place'.

In many households a large brass or copper cover, or 'curfew'—from the French *couvre-feu*—was pushed over the embers at night, and in the morning the fire was restarted with a pair of bellows. Later, of course, a curfew came also to mean a regulation stating that fires had to be extinguished at a certain hour, and people had to stay indoors.

A heavy table of oak planks was the only working surface in the medieval kitchen. The utensils were made of iron, copper or brass and were very heavy and long-lasting. Boiling was the most common method of cooking meat, so pots of all sizes were essential. They were

9 Earthenware pots and an iron skillet

simple and their shape did not change for hundreds, perhaps thousands of years, so it is virtually impossible to date them accurately. As there was no flat surface on which to cook, cauldrons, stewpans, skillets, frying-pans and saucepans either stood on small legs at the edge of the fire, or hung over it from wrought-iron hooks or hangers. Such kitchen terms gradually permeated our language; even as recently as at the beginning of this century, many children were still taught to write by copying out rows and rows of 'pot-hooks' and 'hangers'.

In a large household, with a wide fire, it was useful to be able to vary the position of the pot, according to the heat needed. This was done by means of a 'chimney-crane' or 'pot-crane': this was sometimes just a simple wrought-iron bracket swinging about a rod set in the back wall of the fireplace; sometimes it was a complex piece of mechanism by which the chimney bar could swing, the hook could slide along the bar, and the height of the hook could be adjusted. These cranes were often

very decorative; the main structure was, of course, made to the custo-
mer's own requirements, but the smith used his imagination and skill in
decorating them with twists, curls, scrolls or leaves.

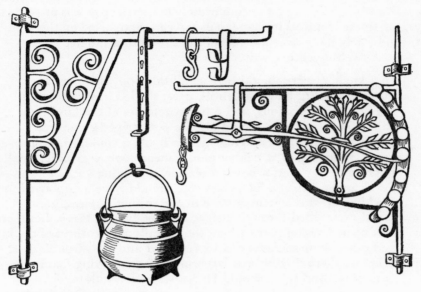

10 Chimney cranes and pot-hangers

    The handles of cooking utensils hanging over a fire were of
course liable to get uncomfortably hot. To avoid injury to the cook's
hands, kettles were often hung on a 'lazy-back' or 'idle-back', an ingenious device which consisted of a rectangular iron frame with a projecting

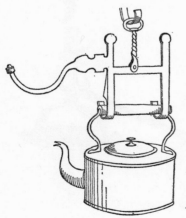

11 Idleback and kettle hanging from a ratchet

handle, so balanced that pressure on the end of the handle caused the kettle to pour without being taken from over the fire.

Frying-pans were almost identical in shape with those we use today, but with longer handles and made of iron. Even the long handle was, however, liable to get uncomfortably hot, so the pan was fitted on to an iron frame identical in shape to its top rim. Supported on this frame, it could safely hang over the side of the fire from a ratchet.

A twelfth-century writer tells us:

> In a kitchen there should be a small table on which cabbage may be minced, and also lentils, peas, shelled beans, beans in the pod, millet, onions, and other vegetables of the kind that can be cut up. There should also be pots, tripods, a mortar, a hatchet, a pestle, a stirring stick, a hook, a cauldron, a bronze vessel, a small pan, a baking pan, a meat-hook, a griddle, small pitchers, a trencher, a bowl, a platter, a pickling vat, and knives for cleaning fish. . . . The chief cook should have a cupboard in the kitchen where he may store many aromatic spices, and bread flour sifted through a sieve may be hidden there. Let there also be a cleaning place where the entrails and feathers of ducks and other domestic fowl can be removed and the birds cleaned. Likewise there should be a large spoon for removing foam and skimming. And there should be hot water for scalding fowl. . . .

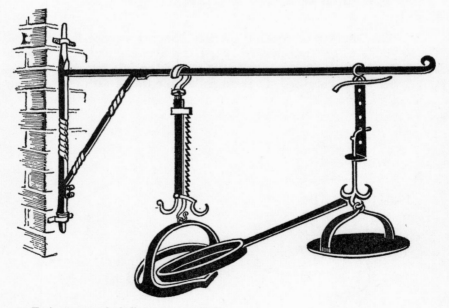

12 Frying-pan and girdlepan on pot-hooks

24

There should be also a garde-robe pit through which the filth of the kitchen may be evacuated. In the pantry let there be shaggy towels, tablecloth, and an ordinary hand towel which shall hang from a pole to avoid mice.

The kitchen of the Paston household at Heylesdon contained the following utensils:

2 doz. pewter vessels
3 pots of brass
2 broaches (spits)
1 marble mortar and 1 pestle
2 pot-hooks
2 brendlets
1 wood axe
4 great brass pans
1 gridiron
1 dressing knife
1 little brass pan holding ½ gallon
2 iron rakes
An almery to keep meat in

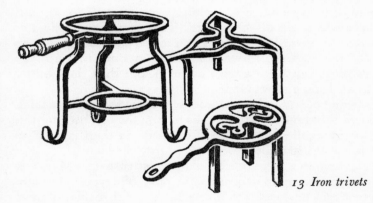

13 Iron trivets

But the buttery, the pantry and the larder were often separate rooms in really large houses. The lack of storage in the hall made it necessary to have some room where the napery, cutlery and glass could be kept. In the Pastons' buttery at Heylesdon they kept, among other things:

6 table cloths
6 towels
12 napkins
6 laten candlesticks

2 silver salts
2 pewter salts
An ale stool
2 pewter basins with 2 ewers
1 barrel vinegar
1 barrel verjuice
12 ale stands
2 pantry knives
A piece of silver plate
12 silver spoons

In large households, on great occasions, the various dishes were carried from the kitchen to the hall with elaborate ceremony by the kitchen servants, who delivered them at the entrance to the hall to other, higher class attendants, who were allowed to approach the tables.

Royalty and high Church dignitaries used gold and silver plates and dishes at table. As there were no banks, and little opportunity for safe investment, gold and silver were always convenient, for they could be melted down and used as exchange if necessary. Dishes were used for serving fish, but meat was often offered on small spits. Dishes seem frequently to have been shared—one between two diners.

In more ordinary households, plates were often of wood, and frequently meat was eaten off 'trenchers'. These were thick slices of bread which were afterwards eaten, or given to the poor, or thrown on to the floor for the dogs. Forks were not used in England until the seventeenth century, but were known about before then, in wealthy households, as an Italian affectation.

The washing of hands at mealtimes was a necessary ceremonial. A servant poured water on the hands of the diners; the jugs used for this were called 'acquamaniles' and were often made in the shape of an animal—when it was tilted the water poured from its mouth.

A curious custom is mentioned in a newsy letter sent by Margaret Paston to her husband on an October day in 1465. She reported to him that 'The mayor and mayoress [of Norwich] sent hither their dinners this day, and John Damme came with them, and they dined here'. There is evidently nothing unusual in this, for Margaret adds: 'I am beholden to them for they have sent to me divers times since ye yed hence.'

Servants were a problem in the Middle Ages, as they always have been, and we find occasional references to thefts of kitchen equipment. John atte Wharf, a citizen of London, had his linen and woollen cloths and 'pots, pails, basins and other things of great value' stolen, but he ultimately found them in St Albans. And Margaret Marcherne, evidently either a kitchen-maid or a waiting-woman at table, took her master's silver and other items to the value of ten pounds.

In large households there were great retinues of servants; men and women of position took pride in surrounding themselves with troops of servants dressed in the livery of the house, and work consequently had to be found for them to do. The household of the Earl of Northumberland, for example, was managed carefully, but he had 166 servants, of whom sixteen attended at table daily. The 'Northumberland Household Book' lists all these men and women, boys and girls, employed in the kitchen, larder, sculleries, bake-houses, brew-houses and dairy, and records their wages.

Servants, like everyone else, were expected to keep their place. A statute of 1363 ordained 'that gromes as well servauntes of lordes . . . shall be served to eate and drinke ones a day of flesshe or of fyshe, and the remenaunte of other vitales, as of mylke, butter, and chese, and other such vitales, accordying to theyr estate'.

Le Ménagier de Paris, a wealthy gentleman, wrote a treatise of instructions for his young wife in 1393. She was only fifteen when they married and he was over sixty, so he gave her many practical instructions on how to engage servants and how to look after them. Good discipline is to be kept, quarrels and bad language prevented, and morals guarded. Each is to have his or her own work assigned, they are to be well but simply fed, but are not to be allowed to sit gossiping at table after meals. The good housewife will see that all her household is in bed early and will—'arrange first that each have beside his bed a candlestick in which to put his candle, and have them wisely taught to extinguish it with the mouth or hand before getting into bed, and by no means with their shirts. . . .' This last would seem to be a rather unnecessary instruction, but evidently the Ménagier did not think so!

A section of John Russell's *Boke of Nurture*, a fifteenth-century book of manners, shows us that the servants had to rearrange tables and seats after a meal, because there was no separate dining room:

> . . . the removal of the Table and separate Service to grand guests in the Chamber, it is instructed . . . thenne uprysying, servitours muste attende to avoyde [clear away] tabills, trestellis, formys and stolys, and to redress bankers [benches] and quyseyons [cushions].

The duties of 'A Pantler or Butler' are also given:

> In the pantry, you must always keep three sharp knives, one to chop the loaves, another to pare them, and a third sharp and keen, to smooth and square the trenchers with. Always cut your lord's bread, and see that it be new; and all other bread at the table one day old ere you cut it, all household bread

three days old, and trencher bread four days old. Look that your salt be fine, white, fair, and dry . . . and see to it that the lid of the salt-cellar touch not the salt. Good son, look that your napery be sweet and clean, and that your table-cloth, towel and napkin be folded exactly, your table-knives brightly polished, and your spoon fair washed—ye wot well what I mean.

The page is told how to perform his various duties:

Put the salt on the right hand of your lord; on its left a trencher or two. On their left a knife, then white rolls, and beside, a spoon folded in a napkin. Cover all up. At the other end set a salt and two trenchers; cut your loaves equal, take a towel $2\frac{1}{2}$ yards long by its ends, fold up a handful from each end, and in the middle of the folds lay eight loaves or buns, bottom to bottom; put a wrapper on the top, twist the ends of the towel together, smooth your wrapper, and open the end of it before your lord.

Instructions are also given for an untrained servant:

Do not claw your head or your back as if you were after a flea, or stroke your hair as if you sought a louse.
Be not glum, nor twinkle with your eyes, nor be heavy of cheer; and keep your eyes from winking and watering.
Do not pick your nose or let it drop clear pearls, or sniff, or blow it too hard, lest your lord hear.
Twist not your neck askew like a jackdaw; wring not your hands with picking or trifling or shrugging, as if ye would saw wood; nor puff up your chest, nor pick your ears, nor be slow of hearing.
Do not have the habit of squirting or spouting with your mouth, or gape or yawn or pout. And do not lick a dish with tongue to get out dust.
Do not sigh with your breast, or cough, or breathe hard in the presence of your sovereign, or hiccough or belch, or groan never the more. Do not trample with your feet, or straddle your legs, or scratch your body. Good son, do not pick your teeth, or grind, or gnash them, or with puffing and blowing cast foul breath upon your lord. . . .

The dairy was, of course, one of the most important parts of the kitchen premises, in households large and small. An Oxfordshire tract, late in the thirteenth century, detailed the duties of a good dairymaid; her final duties seem somewhat odd:

The dairymaid ought to be faithful and of good repute, and

keep herself clean, and ought to know her business and all that belongs to it. She ought not to allow any under-dairymaid or another to take or carry away milk, or butter, or cream, by which the cheese shall be less and the dairy impoverished. And she ought to know well how to make cheese and salt cheese, and she ought to save and keep the vessels of the dairy, that it need not be necessary to buy new ones every year. And she ought to know the day when she begins to make cheese and of what weight, and when she begins to make two cheeses a day, of how much and of what weight, and then the bailiff and the provost ought to inspect the dairy often and the cheeses . . . and no harm done in the dairy, nor any robbery by which the weight shall be lessened. . . . No cow shall be milked or suckled after Michaelmas, and no ewe after the feast of our Lady. . . .
The dairymaid ought to help to winnow the corn when she can be present, and she ought to take care of the geese and hens and answer for the returns and keep and cover the fire, that no harm arise from lack of guard.

Most books of instruction mention the laying of the tablecloth for meals, so we know that this was an important duty. Three cloths seem often to have been laid; perhaps the bottom one reached down to the floor to prevent the domestic animals from walking among the diners' feet. When the cloths were laid, the first thing to be put on the table, and the last thing to be taken off, was the principal salt. This was one of the most elaborate vessels on the table, often in the shape of an ornate ship. Its position on the table determined the seating of the guests: nobles sat 'above the salt', more humble guests below it.

Eating and drinking were among the chief pleasures of life in medieval times. Everyone's food was monotonous, but the difference in diet between rich and poor was very great. In large households a vast amount of time and energy was devoted to the preparation of meals. There was a sudden glut of meat for smoking or salting in the autumn, when cattle had to be killed off because of lack of winter fodder. Christmas was a time of 'large tabling and belly-cheer', after which belts were tightened until the spring. There were more fast days than feast days in the calendar, but those who could afford it were whole-hearted in their feasting. In preparation for Christmas at Winchester Castle in 1206, King John commanded the Sheriff of Hampshire to procure 1,500 chickens, 5,000 eggs, 20 oxen, 100 pigs, and 100 sheep! This was, of course, no ordinary household, but if we remember how slowly and with what difficulties messengers and goods moved about, and when we think of cooking on bonfires, the provision of such meals must indeed have been a feat of organization and improvisation.

14 Medieval feasting

A more modest larder in the year 1311 contained:

The carcasses of twenty oxen, and fifteen pigs, of herrings eight thousand, of dograves [a fish] seven score, twenty pounds of almonds, thirty of rice, six barrels of lard, enough oatmeal to last till Easter, two quarters of salt.

Throughout the Middle Ages it was usual, in wealthy homes, to have two meals a day. The main one, a very large and formal dinner, in the early afternoon; the other, a much lighter supper at which drink seems to have been more important than food. Breakfast consisted only of a snack of bread and ale taken after mass and was not eaten in company. 'Rere suppers', an extra meal taken late in the evening, was condemned by many people as leading to gluttony and lechery. The hours of all meals were largely determined by the season, since the normal household working day ran from sunrise to sunset.

Bartholomaeus Anglicus, a professor of theology at Paris in the thirteenth century, wrote a popular encyclopaedia which dealt with everything from the nature of God to the size of cooking pots. He included instructions on the serving of dinner:

> At feasts, first meat is prepared and arrayed, guests be called together, forms and stools be set up in the hall, and tables, cloths, and towels be ordained, disposed and made ready. Guests be set with the lord in the chief place of the board, and they sit not down at the board before the guests wash their hands. Children be set in their place, and servants at a table by themselves. First knives, spoons and salts be set on the board, and then bread and drink, and many divers messes. Household servants busily help each other to do everything diligently and talk merrily together. The guests are gladded with lutes and harps. Now wine and messes of meat are brought forth and departed. At the last cometh fruit and spices, and when they have eaten, cloths and relief [trestles] are borne away, and guests wash and wipe their hands again. The grace is said, and guests thank the Lord. Then, for gladness and comfort, drink is brought yet again.

Bartholomew 'the Englishman' was an enthusiast for wine. He was convinced that cold water made you ill, especially in old age. He agreed that warm water was good for those who had colic in the night, but declared that wine 'moderately drunk most comforteth the body, and gladdeth the heart, and saveth wounds and evils'.

Early recipes were extraordinarily vague. We, today, are accustomed to cookery books which stress that every ingredient must be weighed and measured, and the heat maintained accurately, but medieval instructions were in such phrases as 'take a bear and seethe him', 'take enough of cinnamon . . . add a good quantity of sugar thereto, put it in an earthen pot and let it boil' and 'boil for so long as it takes to say a Paternoster or a Miserere'. A fifteenth-century cookery book gave instructions how:

> To sley a swan and al mener of foulle and to dight them, tak a swan and cutt hym in the roof of the mouthe toward the brayn of the hed and let hym bled to dethe. Then kep the blod to colour with the chaudron and knyt the nek and let

hym dye. [Again?] Then skald hym, rost hym and serve hym
with chaudron.

Plain food was not appreciated; the aim of cooking was to hash
and chop and pound and spice, and mix ingredients so thoroughly that
nobody could ever be sure what the dish contained. The cook's skill
was in camouflaging and producing something new. In *The Forme of
Cury*, a twelfth-century collection of recipes made by the royal cooks
of King Richard II, most of the recipes for meat, poultry and fish begin
with the admonition to 'smite him to pecys'. The mortar and pestle
were essential items of equipment in the medieval kitchen and there
must have been a constant sound of pounding.

Soups and broths were very popular. In 1542 one writer recorded that 'potage is not so much used in all Christendom as it is used
in England', and mentioned several different kinds of 'potages'—
'stewpottes, grewell, frymentye, pease potage, beane potage, almon
mylke and ryce potage'.

The favourite meat of all classes was pork, and swine, which
had the advantage that they could fend for themselves, were maintained
in large numbers on the mast of oak forests. Each autumn all but a few
animals were killed and salted, and either hung up in the smoke of the
fire to cure, or stored away in great tubs of brine.

Beef and mutton were less popular as food, and the animals
were valued chiefly for drawing the plough and providing leather,
wool and dairy products. Many families must surely have agreed with
the schoolboy who wrote:

I have no delyte in beffe and motyn and such daily metes.
I wolde onys have a partridge set before us, or sum other such,
    and in especiall litell small birdes that I love passyngly well.

Usually meat and fish were not eaten at the same meal. 'Fissche-
dayes' and 'flesche-dayes' were entirely separate; an enormous amount
of fish was eaten, because of the many fish days decreed by Mother
Church. In every week Tuesday, Friday and Saturday were fish days,
together with all Ember Days and the whole of Lent. This must often
have made for very monotonous feeding, as we see from this complaint
by the same dissatisfied schoolboy:

Thou wyll not beleve how wery I am of fyssche and how much
I desir that flesche were cum in ageyn, for I have ete non other
    but salt fyssche this Lent.

Enormous quantities of salt were required in the medieval
kitchen, because of the great emphasis upon preserving meat and fish
and upon the use of souse and brine for pickling. In a large household,
salt was bought by the quarter or the bushel, from local sources as well

as from overseas. It has been suggested that the considerable fluctuations in its price may have been due in large part to the amount of sunshine in each year. Since coastal salt-workers relied on the principle of evaporation, wet years according to this theory would have meant expensive salt; but there were salt-mines also, so supplies would have been supplemented from them.

Perfumed food was popular—perhaps because of the unpleasant smell of high meat. Musk was used in perfuming desserts, and roses, violets, primroses, hawthorn flowers and iris are all mentioned in early recipes.

Spices were prized highly. When the Venerable Bede, Bishop of Durham, lay dying, he distributed his few belongings among his brethren, and divided a little parcel of pepper as one of his most valued possessions.

Chaucer's Franklin liked his sauces 'poinant and sharpe', and most cooks mixed their ingredients freely, but no other recipe that has come down to us stipulated as many spices as that which the Ménagier of Paris decreed for a special preserve. The basis was nuts, turnips, carrots, pears, pumpkins and peaches. The cook was instructed to begin to make the preserve by pounding the nuts on St John's Day (June 24th). For each five hundred nuts there was to be a pound of mustard seed, half a pound of anise, and a quarter and a half each of fennel, coriander and caraway, all pounded and soaked in vinegar. To this hot mixture had to be added half a pound of horse-radish, half a quarter each of cloves, cinnamon, pepper, ginger, nutmeg, grain of paradise, as well as half an ounce of saffron and an ounce of red cedar. All these ingredients were to be mixed with two pounds of mashed raisins, wine and vinegar, and twelve pounds of honey; everything could all be collected by St Andrews Day (November 30th), when the cook was to cook them well. One cannot help wondering where the mixture *stood* for those five months!

15 Sugar loaf and sugar cutters

Sugar was imported into Britain from Syria, Rhodes, Cyprus, Alexandria and Sicily, but for ordinary families the price was prohibitive and honey was used instead. Even a well-to-do housewife like Margaret Paston used sugar only very sparingly, for she wrote to her husband, who was on business in London: 'Bye for mee 1 li of almonds and 1 li of sugar.' Evidently neither was available in Norfolk.

Powdered sugar was a special luxury and was often flavoured with some spice or aromatic flavouring. We read of powdered rose sugar, powdered sugar and powdered mace sugar.

Wealthy households supplemented their diet with ingredients obtained from the East, but these were always expensive because a voyage to Greece through the Mediterranean, or to Russia through the Baltic, was a dangerous and slow affair and the cargo therefore cost a great deal. In the time of Henry III the following kitchen ingredients were listed as imported at the Port of London:

Sugar, cummin, almonds, brazil, quicksilver, ginger, liquorice, small spices, vermilion, glass, figs, raisins, shumac, sulphur, ivory, cinnamon, gingerbread, rice, turpentine, cotton, whalebone, frankincense, pyome, anise, dates, chestnuts, orpiment, olive oil.

It may well be that we have an exaggerated impression of the spiciness of medieval food. It is more than likely that problems of transport and storage may have affected the quality of many imported spices. Most weaken in flavour fairly soon and probably a great quantity was needed in order to achieve a moderate flavour.

Cheese was a staple provision in households, rich and poor. Recipes varied from district to district and in towns many different types could be bought. The dear old Ménagier de Paris explained in verse how cheese should be chosen at market. A good cheese must be:

Not white as snow, like fair Helen,
Nor moist like tearful Magdalen,
Not like Argus, full of eyes,
But heavy, like a bull of prize,
Well resisting a thumb pressed in,
And let it have a scaly skin,
Eyeless, and tearless, in colour not white,
Scaly, resisting, and weighing not light.

It was normal practice among the upper classes to keep household accounts in which the expenses of each day were listed. Sometimes this was done by the lady herself, but a large household would have a steward who was responsible to the lord for all payments made on his behalf. A thirteenth-century judge, Henry de Bracton, wrote a treatise on the laws and customs of England, in which he describes the various functions of the household steward:

It is the steward's duty to account every night in person or through a deputy, with the buyer, marshal, cook, spencer and other officials, for the expenses of the household, and to ascertain the total of the day's expenditures. It is his duty also to take delivery by tally from the larder, at the hands of the reeve, of flesh and fish of every kind as may be necessary, and this he shall have cut up into portions in his presence and counted as they are delivered to the cook and for these he shall hear a reasonable account. It is also his business to know precisely how many farthing loaves can be made from a quarter of wheat, and the pantler is bound to receive this number from the baker. Further he should know how many loaves and how many portions are appropriate for the normal household on ordinary days.

In the public markets the cost of food was strictly regulated and stringent laws ensured reasonable quality. Each town had its own customs and laws which differed from those of others. The word 'by-laws' is derived from the Danish word *by*, meaning a town.

Housewives were always on the lookout for poor quality or under-weight food: watered wine, milk or oil, bread with too much yeast, blown-out meat, stale fish reddened with pig's blood, cheese soaked in broth to make it look richer.

Any butcher who sold bad meat in London was punished by having it burnt in front of his nose as he stood in the pillory unable to move his head. By a proclamation of 1378, London butchers had to close and sell no meat after candles were lighted, as a protection for the public against malpractice. Bakers in particular were closely supervised and liable to be beaten in public if they sold poor or short-weight bread. In 1316 two London bakers were sent to the pillory for making bread of 'false, putrid and rotten materials' and another was 'put upon the pillory, with a whetstone hung from his neck', for falsely saying that his bread, that had been found to be under-weight, had been weighed when cold.

Among lengthy lists of judgements in the City of London in 1419, these would also have been greatly to the satisfaction of all housewives:

Judgement of Pillory upon certain Bakers, who had holes in their tables, called 'moldyngbordes', by means of which they stole their neighbours' dough . . .
Judgement of Pillory for placing a certain piece of iron in a loaf of bread . . .
Judgement of Pillory for selling two stinking capons . . .
Judgement of Pillory for selling oats, good on the outside and the rest bad.

At a time when the population of London was less than 25,000, such simple, open, and very human forms of punishment were probably very effective. In our large, impersonal communities we, of course, have to have a complicated network of central and local regulations, of committees, inspectors, courts and citizens' protection societies.

Many different types of bread were sold in medieval times. The best quality was called 'paindemaigne' or 'manchet' and was often stamped with a figure of Our Lord. Coarse, dark bread was called 'tourte', 'bis', or 'trete'. All types of bread were usually formed in round cakes, like our buns, and these were often marked with a cross. Oatmeal was the staple cereal in the north of England and in Scotland; in the south oats were usually given to horses.

It was of course only in towns that bread was bought from bakers; and even then only by a minority of households. In many towns there were municipal ovens, too, for the use of people who had no oven of their own. Many country people could not afford the luxury of an oven in their homes. The lord of the manor had a bake-house as well as a mill, and the peasants were compelled to bring their dough to the manorial bake-house where, for a fixed charge, it was baked into loaves. The construction of an oven was a skilled and costly job and many peasants' houses were flimsy affairs which were a fire hazard. Later, as houses were built of stone or brick, ovens were built into the structure; eventually every cottage had its own oven and, outside the cities, private baking became general.

We know very little about the domestic life and customs of the poorer classes, that silent majority who could not write and so left no records, who could not afford to have their portraits painted, and often had nothing to leave in a will. There are, however, a few inventories of simple families; in the mid-Essex 'Records' there are occasional references to peasant households, and though there is scarcely any mention of furniture, there is frequent mention of tubs, barrels, vats, troughs and other utensils for making food and drink. Tough but serviceable equipment for cooking was of iron and so evidently passed on from generation to generation, whereas their rough furniture broke sooner and was thrown away or used as firewood, when the owners died.

In *Piers Plowman* it is said that to the poor 'cold flesh and cold fish is to them like baked venison; on Fridays and fasting-days, a farthing's worth of mussels or so many cockles were a feast', and in these verses the author writes so vividly about poverty that one cannot help wondering whether he had not experienced it himself, in that difficult season before harvest-time:

'I have no peny', quoth Piers, 'pullets for to buy
Nor neither geese nor piglets, but two green cheeses,

A few curds and cream and an oaten cake
And two loaves of beans and bran for to bake for my little ones.
And besides I say by my soul I have no salt bacon,
Nor no little eggs, by Christ, collops for to make.
But I have parsley and leeks and many cabbages,
And besides a cow and a calk and a cart mare
To draw afield my dung the while the drought lasteth.
And by this livelihood we must live till lammas time [August]
And by that I hope to have harvest in my croft,
And then I may prepare the dinner as I dearly like.'

There is no reason why we should judge any period by the standards of our own, but if we were suddenly taken back to the Middle Ages we should find a most striking lack of domestic amenities. The nostrils of even the wealthiest people must have been accustomed to a stench which the poorest among us could not tolerate today. Bones and scraps from the tables were thrown on to the floor and, if uneaten by the dogs, lay to rot and, mixed with offal and mud, were later covered with a fresh layer of 'sweet smelling herbs' or rushes.

In spite of frequent municipal decrees, offal and sewage were thrown into the streets and accumulated there until individual householders decided to remove it. In theory, each householder was responsible for keeping the roadway clean in front of his premises. An ordinance of 1383 stated:

And whereas the watercourse of Walbrook is stopped up by divers filth and dung thrown therein by persons who have houses along the said course, to the great nuisance and damage of all the city . . . punishment may be inflicted upon the offenders . . . But it shall be fully lawful for those persons who have houses on the said watercourse, to have latrines over the course, provided that they do not throw kitchen or other refuse through the same, whereby the passage of the said water may be stopped.

And in 1421 one William atte Wode was accused 'for making a great nuisance and discomfort to his neighbours by throwing out horrible filth, on to the highway, the stench of which is so odious that none of his neighbours can remain in their shops.'

Another public nuisance of domestic origin was caused from time to time by people who made linen by soaking and shredding the tissues of the hemp plant, and so causing objectionable fumes. We are apt to forget that relatively few social problems are new; there is a strangely modern ring about a medieval law which stated:

We are disposed to preserve by our zealous solicitude . . . the salubrious air which divine judgement has provided. We therefore command that henceforth no one is permitted to place linen or hemp for retting in any waters within the distance of one mile from any city or castle, lest for this the quality of the air is corrupted.

People washed very little and nobody thought of having baths regularly. Here are complicated instructions to a servant for preparing a bath for his master when he is not well:

Boil together hollyhock, mallow, wall pellitory, and brown fennel, danewort, St John's wort, centuary, ribwort, and camomile, heyhove, hayriff, herbbenet, bresewort, smallage, water speedwell, scabious, bugloss and wild flax which is good for aches. Boil withy leaves and great oats together with them, and throw them into a vessel and put your lord over it and let him endure it for a while as hot as he can, being covered over and closed on every side; and whatever disease, grievance or pain ye be vexed with, this medicine shall surely make you whole, as men say.

Ideas of propriety were different from those of today. Many medieval pictures show servants serving meals to their lord and lady sitting in the bath! Babies were bathed in large iron cauldrons or kettles, which were also used for cooking and laundry.

There were very few doctors in the Middle Ages and most medicines were made at home in the kitchen. Herbs were much used, and some of the remedies seem to us absurd, such as putting a wreath of the plant penny-royal round your head as a cure for headache, or giddiness, and rubbing raw onion into the bite caused by a mad dog. Sleeping draughts are frequently mentioned; one mixture consisted of hemlock, opium, mulberry juice, hyoscyamus, ivy, mandragora and lettuce, dried on a sponge. When moistened it was inhaled by the patient, who was afterwards roused by fennel juice applied to the nostrils.

For a headache you should 'take a vessel full of leaves of green rue, and a spoonful of mustard seed, rub together, add the white of an egg, a spoonful, that the salve may be thick. Smear with a feather on the side that is sore.'

Some of these remedies were effective, but certainly modern psychologists would say that the effort and activity involved in applying even those that were pharmacologically useless could nevertheless be very beneficial to a patient. The housewife had to be nurse, doctor and psychologist too.

Nowadays we are apt to forget how much of a businesswoman

she also had to be. It was not only necessary to arrange and see that the house was kept clean, according to the current ideas of cleanliness, and to provide enough palatable food for everyone, but the housewife had also to arrange for her supplies. She had to think ahead and to preserve and store and buy and spin and sew, in order to have the necessities ready when needed. A lack of forethought on her part would mean a lack of something important for her family several months later.

16 Spinning and carding wool

The ladies of a wealthy household spent a great deal of time spinning, at first on a distaff and later on a spinning wheel. A distaff was a wooden rod on one end of which a rough mass of sheep's wool was fastened; a little of this was drawn out at a time and twisted between finger and thumb to form a thread which was wound on to a spindle. Every woman had her own distaff, and most girls too. Sometimes we read that they were used as weapons, when there was a quarrel in the family!

Because the unmarried women in the home had time to do a good deal of the spinning, they came to be called 'spinsters'; the name has outgrown its original meaning, as often happens.

In his Prologue to *The Wife of Bath's Tale*, Chaucer seems to imply that spinning was a blessing, but it must often have seemed a dreadful, unending chore:

Deceive weeping, spinning God hath given
To women kindly while they may liven.

Not only spinning and weaving, but the actual cutting out and making up of garments and household gear occupied a great deal of time. Margaret Paston apologizes in one of her letters because she has no time to get some material made up into shirts for her son. She writes: 'I should have got them made here, but that should have been

39

too long ere you should have had them. Your aunt, or some other good woman, will do them.'

The lady of a castle or large manor house had to train not only the many servants of her household and her own young children, but also older boys and girls sent for that purpose from neighbouring great houses.

A series of 'Books of Nurture' were written for the education of young people of good family serving in a humble capacity in a great household. Most of the books were written by men, for the instruction of boys, and this reflects the fact that household staff in the Middle Ages apparently consisted almost entirely of men and boys. Thomas à Becket, when Chancellor of England, had a number of boys living in his house and working in his kitchens. Women and girls were in attendance upon the ladies of the household, but apparently did no domestic work.

Many writers of books of etiquette of the time stress the necessity of correct deportment when serving in a strange household. Human nature being, in the Middle Ages, what it was before and has been ever since, these young boys and girls must often have been a burden to their hostesses and a complication in even the best run household.

To most people today 'to starve' means to want for food, but in earlier times it meant also 'to starve with cold'. Medieval castles and manor houses were probably even colder and draughtier than peasants' cottages, where the inhabitants had at least the comfort of living and sleeping in a cosy fug. Window glass was too rare and expensive for domestic use, even in grand households, so 'wind-eyes' were either open to the elements or roughly covered with thin plates of horn or oiled canvas. Shutters on opposite windows might allow some uncertain control of the draught according to the direction of the wind, and the art of judging how the wind would blow was among the necessary qualifications of a cook.

17 Lanterns of horn and metal

People lived in darkness as much as in cold. Lanterns made of horn or torches of twisted hemp dipped in tallow were carried by servants in the house and out of doors. Candles were expensive and only used in grand households and for church services. Tallow-candle-makers plied their trade from house to house in the towns, making candles out of the clarified mutton fat saved in the kitchens. There were huge flocks of sheep—up to two thousand strong—grazing in wool-rearing areas of England, and there must have been tallow enough, in those parts of the country, for even modest homes. In his *Good Huswives Day* Thomas Tusser refers to tallow candles:

Wife make thine owne candle
Provide for thy tallow ere frost cometh in
And make thine owne candle ere winter begin.

The light most easily afforded by the poor was the rush dipped in tallow. In autumn servants or children were sent to gather rushes from the banks of rivers and streams; they then laid them aside to dry. Some were strewn on the floor to give quiet and a little warmth, and to cover the dirt and offal lying there. Others were peeled, cut into lengths of about a foot and dipped several times into hot melted fat which had dripped from the spit during cooking, into an iron 'grease-pan'. After each dipping the rush was left to dry, so that each new layer of fat stuck on to the one underneath, until the rush looked very much like a modern taper. They were then held in metal clips on wooden stands, called 'rush-nips' or 'rush-holders'. A rushlight burned for about half an hour, but if extra light were needed the rush could be put into the nip in such a way that both ends could be lit at the same time. This, of course, halved the burning time and doubled the number of rushes required; an extravagant way of going on which gave rise to the phrase 'burning the candle at both ends'.

It was all a very laborious business and it is not surprising that bedtime in humble homes was early, that servants were severely rationed for lights, and that domestic work was done mainly during the daylight hours.

We do not read much about house-cleaning in the Middle Ages, or indeed for a long time after that, but rooms were presumably cleaned from time to time. While the hall and the solar were the only rooms of any consequence, and while furniture was only minimal, little cleaning work could have been involved. But gradually, as a desire for a greater comfort and privacy caused the wealthy to build all manner of new service rooms and sleeping quarters, the responsibilities of maintaining the home increased. Small mops made of bunches of heather and brooms of birch or willow twigs were used for what little house-cleaning was done.

41

All the kitchen utensils and equipment had to be cleaned with black soap—a mixture of sand, sifted ashes and linseed oil. Fine toilet soap was scented with herbs in the kitchen or still-room and kept in wooden bowls. Laundering was a large-scale, periodic affair which seems to have taken place outside in good weather and was doubtless, in a large ménage, an occasion of friendly frolic and noise.

Laundresses sometimes used fuller's earth, which was white clay and a strong alkaline solution, made from ash, called lye. There was often trouble about domestic washing. In 1120 the women washing in the brook at Reading made such a disturbance with their battledores, beating their washing, that the burghers in the new guildhall complained. And at Sandwich, in Kent, the common serjeant had to take special care to prevent washerwomen from rinsing clothes in the public stream.

The laundress was an indispensable servant in every large household, though she was one of the poorest paid. Petronilla, the laundress of Simon de Montfort's household in the thirteenth century, does not appear in the yearly accounts, though she did receive a pair of shoes worth 12 pence, and payment of 15 pence on May 31st 1265, for laundry work done since the new year.

Furs and woollen clothes were periodically beaten, shaken and carefully looked over. A special cleaning fluid was made of wine, lye, fuller's earth and the juice pressed from green grapes. Grease stains were soaked in warm wine or rubbed with chicken feathers rinsed in hot water. Faded colours could be restored by rubbing with a sponge soaked in diluted lye, and damp furs were sprinkled with wine and flour and allowed to dry before being brushed over.

Fleas were a very common trial in the Middle Ages. The Ménagier instructed his young wife in several different ways of getting rid of them:

> If the room be scattered with alder leaves the fleas will get
> caught therein . . . if you have at night one or two trenchers of
> bread covered with birdlime or turpentine and put about the
> room with a lighted candle set in the midst of each trencher,
> they will come and get stuck thereto. . . . I have seen blankets
> placed on the straw and on the bed and when the black fleas
> jumped upon them they were the sooner found and killed upon
> the white. . . .

The Ménagier writes vividly about the duties of a housewife in caring for her husband's creature comforts. This part of his book is particularly touching, because the old man is telling his wife how to look after his successor—'another husband after me':

Cherish the person of your husband carefully, and I pray you,

keep him in clean linen, for 'tis your business . . . to have his
shoes removed before a good fire, his feet washed and to have
fresh shoes and stockings, to be given good food and drink, to
be well served and well looked after, well bedded in white
sheets and night-caps. . . . And therefore I counsel you to make
such cheer of your husband and to be peaceable with him and
remember the rustic proverb, which saith that there be three
things which drive the goodman from home, to wit a dripping
roof, a smoking chimney and a scolding woman.

He likens the wife's love for her husband to the fidelity of domestic animals towards their masters:

Of the domestic animals you see how a greyhound, or a mastiff,
or a little dog, whether on the road, or at table, or in bed,
always keeps near the person from whom he takes his food . . .
and is shy and fierce with all others . . . he always has his heart
and his eye upon his master; even if his master whip him and
throw stones at him, the dog follows, wagging his tail and lying
down before his master . . . wherefore for a better and stronger
reason women, to whom God has given natural sense and who
are reasonable, ought to have a perfect and solemn love for
their husbands.

18 A medieval vineyard

In view of the great domestic discomforts of these times we can easily understand the poets' outbursts of joy at the approach of spring. The young season is welcome in any country where winter is desolate and cold, but the medieval poet in northern Europe was celebrating, in addition, the joyous fact that he was no longer confined to the house by severe weather, that the sun had dried the roads and made them passable again, that he no longer had to huddle himself in heavy clothing indoors, and that soon there would be an end to the monotonous diet of salted meat and salted fish. Kitchen life and work also broke into new life when winter was over. 'Spring' cleaning was afoot and 'Sumer is icumen in', written in 1250, must have echoed relief and joy felt in every English household.

6

The Sixteenth Century

In the records of Hampton Court Palace there is mention of the great kitchen, the privy kitchen, and also the cellar, larder, pantry, buttery, scullery, ewery, saucery, chaundry, spicery, poultery, victualling house and many other offices. But of course Hampton Court was never a typical household.

Of more detailed interest is the description of a yeoman's house given in his will of 1571. In it he made provision for his wife in a curious way:

> I geve and bequeve to Agnys my wyfe enduringe the tyme of her naturall lyfe my parler in the weste syde of my house at Lythehill wch adionethe to the hawle there, the chamber over the same parler, the garret above the same chamber, the lofte over the hawle and the kytchen lofte with free ingres, egress and regres. Roome and fyer in the said hawle at all tymes and also halfe the kytchen, and fyer boote to dresse meate and drincke, bake and brewe, and to doe all other necessaryes mete and convenyent in the same kytchen at all tymes and halfe the newe coope nowe standinge in the sayde kytchen . . . all my pewter vessyll . . . my beste and my leaste twoe candlestycke, my beste brasse potts, my beste and my leaste twoe kettles, my posnet of belle brasse, my leaste skyllet of brasse . . . halfe my bakon at the beame (excepte the twoe greatests flytches and the twoe leaste flytches), halfe my larde and greace, twoe of the beste flytches of dryed beefe, twoe of my beste table clothes, twoe of my beste towels, halfe of all my table napkyns, one dozen of my beste spones, my three beste cuppes. . . .

Most people were wanting to improve their houses at this time, if they could afford to. A second room might be added to a one-room cottage; a 'chamber' might be made out of a hayloft; workrooms or additional living rooms were added on to manor houses; and many fine mansions were built. Here a proud owner shows a friend round the kitchen department of his new house:

> These buildings severed from the rest do serve as guest chambers with a chamber for my hothouse. My owne lodging . . . is built upon higher ground, both for the better air and fayer prospect. . . . The windows for the most part open all East and some South. . . . Here is my larder built with three rooms, one serving for butter and milk, one for beer and wine and the third to keep flesh of all kinds, poudered [salted] and unpoudered, and fowles of all sorts, with convenient hooks to hang them up from trouble. Above is a corn loft, with floor of stone and plaster wall, and an apple close. Here is a Bakehouse, and a pantrie with two ovens, one serving for household bread and the other for manchet loaves for my own table, and for tarts and fine bakemeats. Here are also troughs to keep meale in and troughs to lay leaven in and there is a fair table to mould upon.

It is virtually impossible to get any real idea of the household expenses of the average working man. The value of money was totally different from what it is today, people's needs were in many ways

19 Mortar and pestle, nutmeg grater and spice box

simpler, and they knew nothing of many things which we consider essential. Here are the expenses of a baker, which were listed as evidence that he was running his business at a loss:

Weekly expenses:	£	s	d
House rent at £30 per annum		11	6
Diet of a man and wife 10/–; of 3 children 7/–		17	0

Diet of 4 journeymen 2 apprentices and 3 maids at 4/–	1	12	0
Clothing of man wife and apprentice at £20 per annum		7	8
Clothing and schooling of 3 children		3	0
Wages of 4 journeymen at 2/6; of 2 maids at 10d		11	8
Yeast 10/– wood 12/– coal 1/4 sacks 1/– water 8d boulters 1/– garner rent 2/– baskets 3d salt 1/–	1	9	3
Miller's toll 15/– porters' fees 2/–		17	0
Parson, Poor rate, scavenger, Watch		1	0
Total expense of baking 6 quarters of wheat into bread	£6	10	1

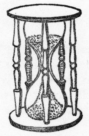

20 Hour-glass

English people have always been noted as great eaters. A sixteenth-century writer commented, 'Our English cannot live by roots, by water herbs or such beggary baggage', and complained that the great rise in the price of meat meant that ordinary people could not afford to buy it. But this list of the meals eaten by a well-to-do bachelor in his lodgings in London in 1589 suggests that expectations were high:

> May 11, dinner:
>
> | | |
> |---|---|
> | A piece of beef | 18d |
> | A loin of veal | 2s |
> | 2 chickens | 13d |
> | Oranges | 2d |
> | For dressing the veal and chicken and service | 12d |
>
> . . . and for supper the same day:
>
> | | |
> |---|---|
> | A shoulder of mutton | 16d |
> | 2 rabbits | 10d |
> | For dressing the mutton and rabbits and a pig's pettitoes | 8d |
> | Cold beef | 8d |
> | Cheese | 2d |

... and on June 20th, when he must surely have had friends to dinner:

Butter	4d
A piece of beef	14d
A leg of mutton	18d
A loin of veal	22d
2 pecks of peascods	8d
3 rabbits	2s
A quart of cream	6d
3 quarts of strawberries	16d
2 lb of cherries	20d
½ lb of musk confects	11d
Oranges	3d
2 lemons	6d
Bread	8d
Beer	9d

In a large household open house was kept for a variety of lesser people, as well as for formal entertaining of relatives and friends. There was, of course, no public transport service, so if a workman or a delivery man came to the house he came on foot or on horseback, and it was reasonable for him to expect to be given refreshment or, sometimes, a night's lodging.

The kitchen books, or 'week books' of the household of Sir William Petre, Secretary to the King, living at Ingatestone Hall in Essex, have been preserved and are among the few surviving records of the food and drink consumed in a mid-sixteenth-century manor house of moderate size. It is recorded that, during the year 1552, a number of Sir William's tenants ate in the Hall every week and there were also regular visits by local craftsmen—tiler, smith, glazier, wheelwright, sawyer, bricklayer, and carpenter, in addition to unskilled labourers. We know that from August to October six carpenters, a tailor and a maltman ate at Ingatestone; four carters brought oats and were given food; and ten carters 'that came with pale from Writtle'. Pedlars appear from time to time, there were also paupers—a few 'poor folks' or 'poor fellows'. On Christmas Day 1551 there is mention of 'a mess in the hall and three poor fellows that came from London'. (A mess consisted of four people served with meat.) One Sunday there were 'eight poor folks, besides two mess that came unbid', and on another occasion 'four singers and players'. As all food provided had to be accounted for by the steward, we can assume that the record of hospitality is reasonably accurate.

As always, a large house required a large number of servants to maintain it, most of whom were centred round the kitchen. The house-steward was the head servant, often assisted by an 'acater', or buyer, who was responsible for acquiring the considerable supplies needed. In Sir William Petre's establishment the steward made a weekly visit of inspection to the granaries, mill-house, malt-house, bake-house, dairy, dovecot, and the various storerooms of cheese, fish, and so on. He and the cook inspected the larders and the pantries. Each Saturday he wrote in his kitchen book a statement of what provisions had been received, how much was spent, and how much remained in store.

In country districts servants were hired at the annual fairs; in London servants would put up advertisements on the pillars of the nave of St Paul's Cathedral. Shakespeare's Falstaff, referring to a servant, says, 'I bought him in Paul's'.

In addition to their wages, servants had free board and lodging and their livery allowance of clothing. Every spring and autumn there would be a bulk purchase of cloth for liveries, to be made up by sewing-maids or by the 'gentlewomen' under the watchful eye of the lady of the house. The maids often made the ordinary clothes for the family, as well as their own. A certain amount of the actual cloth for everyday garments was made at home. In the kitchen books of Ingatestone Hall we find occasionally such references as 'spinning 4 lb tow, 8d', 'spinning 1 lb fine flax, 6d' and 'weaving 37 ells fine canvas, 18s 6d'.

The costume of servants was regulated by law, though citizens could now wear whatever they liked.[1] Maidservants were not permitted to wear lawn, cambric, tiffany or fine linen on their heads, and their headgear should not be trimmed with lace. Their kerchiefs were to be plain, but they were allowed to wear ruffs so long as these did not exceed four yards in length 'before the gathering or setting thereof, nor three inches in depth within the setting in thereof'. Gowns and kirtles were not to be made of any kind of silk or of kersey which cost above three shillings a yard. Farthingales were strictly forbidden, 'either little or great'. But the regulations were often disobeyed—as one would expect—for the Lord Mayor of London (of all people!) complained to the Grocers' Company of 'the inordynate pryde of mayde servauntes and women servauntes in their excess of apparell and follye in varietie of newe fashions . . .'

Servants were treated badly or well according to the temperament and standards of their master and mistress. There is a record of a Wiltshire maid who complained before the magistrates of having her collar-bone and two ribs broken by her angry mistress, but this must have been very rare.

William Harrison, in his *Description of England,* published in 1587, tells us that servants often slept on the floor:

---

[1] In previous centuries Sumptuary Laws had been strict, and laid down what each person should wear, according to his or her position in society.

We ourselves have lyen full oft upon straw pallettes, covered
only with a sheet, under coverlet made of dogswain or
hop-harlots and a good round logge under our heads, instead of
a boulster. . . . As for servants, if they had any sheetes above
them, it was well, for seldome had they any under their bodies,
to keepe them from the prickinge straws that ranne oft thorow
the canvas, and rased their hardened hides.

There was nothing inferior in being a servant. The word implied
a 'servitor'—somebody who served, or helped, somebody else. If you
were a kitchen boy, a turnspit or a laundry-maid you were a servant,
but so were the chaplain and the nobleman's son who waited at table.
They were gentlemen by birth and education, but because they 'served'
they were servants.

Children were still placed as pages, or other servants, in noble
households away from their own homes, just as they had been in
medieval times. They provided constant attention to their masters and
mistresses, and received at the same time a general education until they
were fifteen or sixteen years old.

Between seven and eight in the morning a groom and a page had
to be ready to serve in the great hall. Before then the pages had to take
up their straw pallets on which they had slept and clear away those of the
squires and knights. They had to clean the floors, strew them with fresh
rushes, light the fires, and shake the tapestries. The rushes had always
to be strewn before the tapestries were rehung, so as not to spoil them
with dust.

Sir Thomas More was undoubtedly a kindlier and more loving
employer than others of his time, and there is a touching evidence of his
thought for his servants. In the last of the affectionate letters he wrote to
his daughter Margaret Roper, his 'derlyng Megg', he added:

I like speciall well Dorothy Colley, I pray you be good to her.
I would wit whether this be she that you wrote me of. If not,
I pray you be good to the other as you may in her affliction,
and to Joan Aleyn too. Give her I pray you some kind answer,
for she sued hither to me this day to pray you be good to her.

Servants were often remembered in wills. Sir Francis Drake, who
maintained a retinue appropriate to the Queen's General at Sea, left
£20 apiece to four of his menservants, to others 'beinge of the better
sorte, tenn poundes of lawfull English monie', to those 'beinge of the
second sorte' £5, and 'to the residue of all my common servantes, both
men and women, which shall be serving in my house at the time of my
death and departure, to each of them the sum of fortie shillings'.

Many bequests were not in money, but in kind. In 1521 one Robert Frevyll of Ely left 'To Jane Colyne, my servant, a quarter of barley; to Jane Barker, my servant, three quarters of barley, four sheep, and a pair of sheets'. One is tempted to wonder what additional services the second Jane had rendered her master!

A charming picture of a maid is given in verses by Thomas Churchyard:

She wanne the love of all the house,
And pranckt it like a pretty mouse;
And sure at every word she spake
A goodlie curtchie would she make.
She sweeped under every bench
And shaekt the coshens in their kinde.
When out of order did she find
A rush, a straw, or little stick,
She could it mend, she was so quicke
About her business every houre:
This maide was cald her mistres' floure.

We get a glimpse of the varied duties of servants in Chester Castle in a letter which the Governor's wife sent thanking a friend for

21 Preparing for a feast

obtaining two maids for her: 'The work I have for them is the chamber to look to, and pewter to rub, and the washing of my finer linen . . . and brewing and baking . . . and the scouring of all my pewter once a week . . . and attending to the dairy and the piggery'. Her letter does not suggest that the girls had much time off.

The sheer variety of work which centred round the kitchen must have made life eventful and interesting. Even the youngest kitchen maid could feel that she was one of a team, helping to maintain an inter-dependent community of people. Not all mistresses or masters were kind or even reasonable, and many servants probably skimped their work while they gossiped, or stayed out later than was permitted, but it is certain that nobody could have been bored. Machines to 'save' work were centuries ahead and work filled most people's lives.

However many servants she might have, the mistress of a great household had much to do herself. Lady Hoby was evidently a pious and efficient lady who kept her women servants busy by her own example:

> After private prayer I saw a man's leg dressed, took order for things in the house and wrought [sewed?] till dinner time. . . .
> Went about my stilling; stilled aqua vitae.
> Gave a poor woman a salve for her arm.
> After breakfast I was busy to dye wool.
> I was visited by a kinswoman, which was some trouble at first, but considering all crosses, ought thankfully to be borne.
> I did busy myself about making of oil in my closet.
> Bought a little spinning wheel and span of that.
> After dinner I was busy weighing of wool till almost night.
> Busy about wax lights. I did see lights made almost all the afternoon.
> I went to take my bees and saw my honey ordered.
> After I dined I talked and read to some good wives.
> I walked with Mr. Hoby about the town, to spy out the best places where cottages might be builded.

Every housewife, whether of high or middling station, had her herb-garden, her still-room and her book of tried recipes. Herb-gathering was a regular occupation and there was probably a certain amount of rivalry between the maids, to see who was permitted to help the mistress prepare medicines, cosmetics and domestic dyes.

It was part of the ordinary education of a gentlewoman to know how to prepare and administer simple drugs and remedies. Often, for good or ill, the lady of the manor would doctor the whole village with her syrups and salves. Countrywomen grew herbs in their cottage gardens and sold them to those who wanted to make up their own cordials.

Such wild plants as camomile, betony, borage, cowslips and tormentil were much used and few gardens were without balm, rosemary and peonies, as well as the usual culinary herbs.

Here are two recipes for cures:

> The head of a dragon keepeth one from looking a squint and if set up at the gates and doors it hath been thought in ancient times to be very fortunate to the sincere worshippers of God.

> The eyes of dragons, kept till they be stale and afterwards beat into an oil with honey and made into an ointment, keep anyone that useth it from the terror of night visions and apparitions.

And two ways of making toothpaste, also a home product:

> To keep the teeth both white and sound, take a quart of honey, as much vinegar and half as much white wine, boil them together and wash your teeth therewith now and then.
> The heads of mice, burned, are said to make an excellent powder for the scouring and cleansing of the teeth, called tooth soap.

Dr Andrew Boorde who wrote his *Dyetary of Helthe* in 1542 thought that 'no man should enterpryse to meddle with physic but they which be learned and admitted', but many people had much more faith in simple home remedies than all the bleedings, salves and purges of physicians.

Gardens were laid out in formal, architectural patterns, with 'knots' or beds in elaborate symmetrical shapes. New herbs, shrubs, flowers and fruit were constantly being brought to England by travellers. In his *Description of England,* published in 1587, Harrison remarked on the apricots, almonds, peaches and figs as 'strange fruit'. Oranges were sometimes called 'portynggales' (Portuguese oranges). This is the first book we have dealing with the preparation of food and its consumption in a general way. Earlier books were 'bokes of kervynge' dealing with table etiquette.

Even the smallest cottages had gardens full of herbs and vegetables. Stocks, pinks and marigolds were grown for preserving in vinegar and sugar as winter 'sallats'. In one household book, there is mention, at the end of the century, of a large expenditure on seeds of chives, sweet marjoram, purslane, cauliflower and mustard, and of thirty-five bushels of lime bought for the kitchen-garden.

In Sir William Petre's orchard, in a sheltered south-west corner, there was 'the banqueting house well and fair builded'. This was a summer house or small pavilion in which the 'banquet'—the final sweet or fruit course—was served to guests when the weather was kind.

Nearby was a walled enclosure which contained 'the cook's garden', a 'brick dove-house well replenished with doves', and one of many ponds well stocked with fish always ready for the table.

In Tudor times everyone thought of small birds as edible, just as many continental people do today. The choicest dish was of larks, and several dozens of them are referred to on occasions in the kitchen-books of Ingatestone Hall. On one occasion a neighbour sent a present of a crane, seven dozen larks and seven 'snites'. In the accounts a 'birder' often appears as being paid for wildfowl, sparrows, blackbirds, starlings and thrushes. The pigeon-loft was still a prominent feature of the farm-yard of big estates. It housed hundreds of birds and provided a source of fresh meat through the winter.

Pets were an important part of the household and the English were notorious in Europe for their devotion to dogs and horses. These were mainly for hunting deer; the favourite indoor animals were cats, which seem to have been little different from ours according to this charming description:

> This beast is wonderful nimble, setting upon her prey like a lion, by leaping. She huntest both rats, all kinds of mice and birds, eating not only them but fish, wherewithal she is best pleased. It is needless to spend any time writing about her loving nature to man, how she flattereth by rubbing her skin against one's legs, how she whirleth with her voice, having as many tunes as turns, for she hath one voice to beg and complain, another to show her delight and pleasure, another among her own kind by flattering, by hissing, by puffing, by spitting . . . she beggeth, playeth, leapeth, looketh, catcheth, tosseth with her foot, riseth up to strings held over her head, sometimes creeping, sometimes lying on the back. . . .

Very little water was drunk and the physician, Dr Boorde, wrote that 'water is not wholesome sole by itself for an Englishman'. Ale was drunk by everyone, young and old; hops were introduced in 1525 and after then 'single beer', 'household beer' or 'March beer' were drunk in most households. Brewing was normally the housewife's responsibility, but a great house would employ a brewer, either full- or part-time. The brewing equipment at Ingatestone Hall consisted of rowers (in which to stir the barley), a scavel (shovel), jets (large ladles), a mashing vat (in which hot water was added to the malt), a sweet wort tun, a copper for boiling wort, a cooler, a chunk (into which the wort ran), a yealding vat (in which the wort was left to ferment), cowls (big tubes), yeast-tuns, yeast-casks, leaded troughs, skeps (baskets), a stuke and a pulley (for loading the casks to be carted to the buttery), and vats and casks of all kinds and sizes.

Vineyards had been characteristic of the great religious houses in England in the Middle Ages and large amounts of wine, mainly white, had been drunk until the sixteenth century. The dissolution of the monasteries dispersed those who had kept alive the art of tending the vines, and the vineyards disappeared. Grapes were grown only in the gardens of a few noble households.

French and Rhenish wines were imported in large quantity and the Ingatestone Hall stocktaking in December 1551 reveals:

A butt of sack and 12 gallons
2 puncheons of French wine and 20 gallons
An hogshead of French wine
An hogshead of Gascon wine with an half
An hogshead of red wine with an half
A piece of Rhenish wine
4 gallons of malmsey

All wines were drunk 'from the wood'—that is, they were stored in wooden casks and the bottles, fitted with a wooden peg, were filled

22 *Earthenware pitcher, horn mug and pewter mug*

just before being put on the table. Cork-bark stoppers, to provide a lasting seal to the bottle, were not introduced until late in the seventeenth century.

The cellar at Ingatestone Hall also contained verjuice, a kind of sharp cider used in cooking, and perry—both made at home in the kitchen. Mead and various flower and fruit wines were made in more modest households. A foreigner who visited this country in 1599 wrote that in some parts of England 'we were given nothing but milk to drink in tankards instead of beer'. All drinks were served in pewter tankards, stoneware mugs, or in the black leather jacks of medieval days.

Tableware was of wood or pewter; wooden bowls were still in use in simple households. Square or round wooden platters were often reversed: you ate one course on one side and turned it over for the second.

Special circular plates called 'roundels' were used on special occasions. They were usually of wood cut very thin and decorated on one side with painted verses. The plain side was used during a meal and afterwards the poems were read out or sung by the guests. A set of roundels in the Victoria and Albert Museum shows drawings of a monkey, a cat, a thief and a dog, and written round the edge are these uplifting verses:

> The monkey seeing nutts in fyre
> Doth force the cat to plucke them hyer
> This shews ye envious not to care
> Whose howse do burn for ye have share
> False theves with breade the dogges allay
> Theire masters householde do betray
> This warneth us from bribes to fly
> Leste that we hurte our friends thereby.

William Harrison compared the eating habits of the past with those common in his day. Much more time used to be spent in the past in eating and drinking, 'for whereas of old we had breakfasts in the forenoon, beverages or nunchions after dinner, and thereto rear-suppers generally when it was time to go to rest, now these odd repasts, thanked be God, are very well left, and each one in manner contenteth himself with dinner and supper only.'

Harrison tells us that gentry and students dined at eleven and supped between five and six 'at afternoon'; the merchants at twelve and six; husbandmen at noon and seven or eight; university scholars dine at ten. And he adds: 'As for the poorest sort they generally dine and sup when they may, so that to talk of their order of repast it were but a needless matter.'

By the middle of the century the lord and his family no longer dined in the hall with members of the household, but apart in a smaller room called a 'winter parlour' or 'dining parlour'. Important visitors were entertained in the 'dining chamber'.

Waiting at table was an important skill which had to be learned by anyone employed in a grand house. These instructions were evidently given to a beginner, who had, perhaps, first been working as a kitchen servant:

> When your master will go to his meat, cover your table and
> set on salt, bread, and trenchers, the salt before the bread,
> the trenchers before the salt, and set your napkins and spoons
> upon the cupboard ready and lay every man a trencher and

napkin and a spoon. And some do use to set before every man
a loaf of bread and his cup. Also see you have voiders in
readiness for to avoid [empty out] the morsels that they do
leave on their trenchers. Then with your trencher knife take off
such fragments and put them in your voider and set them clean
again. And when men have well eaten and do begin to wax
weary of eating, you shall take up the meat and void the table,
and then set down cheese or fruits. Notice if your master is used
to wash at the table or standing and cast a clean towel upon
your table-cloth and set down your ewer and basin before him.

In a *Booke of Nurture,* published in 1568, we find equally precise instructions about the preparation of a bed:

When your master intends to bedward, see that you have
fire and candle sufficient and see that you have clean water
in at night and in the morning and if your master lie in fresh
sheets, dry off the dankness by the fire; then fold down his
bed and warm his night-kerchief, help off his clothing and
draw the curtains.

When guests came to stay the visit generally lasted for several
weeks, or even months, and much preparation was of course necessary
in the kitchen. When Queen Elizabeth went to stay with Sir George
More at Loseley in 1583, he and his family had to go away so as to
leave room for the Queen and her retinue.

One fashionable article of clothing which gave rise to a great
deal of work in the sixteenth-century kitchen was the ruff. By the end of
the century men and women, boys and girls, all wore ruffs; the larger
they were, and the smarter, the more they had to be washed, starched
and ironed.

Starching was a messy business. Starch was made from rice
mixed with size and seems usually to have been bought and not made
at home—perhaps because of the smell. In 1614 there was a complaint
made against a starch-maker in Essex, whose business 'caused such a
stink and ill-favour so that subjects were not able to come and go along
the highway without great danger to their lives and through the
loathesome smell.'

Candle-making was an important job too. For the simplest
candles a twisted cloth wick had to be dipped into fat a great many
times; later, they were made by pouring fat into moulds in which the
wicks had previously been fixed. Candles were made in many sizes and,
if bought, they were ordered by weight. A merchant's wife living near
London in the early years of the century ordered: 'For my candles, I
pray you make me 24 dozen. I would have, of 4 in the lb, 1 in the lb
and 8 in the lb, of each 4 dozen, and the rest of smaller sorts.'

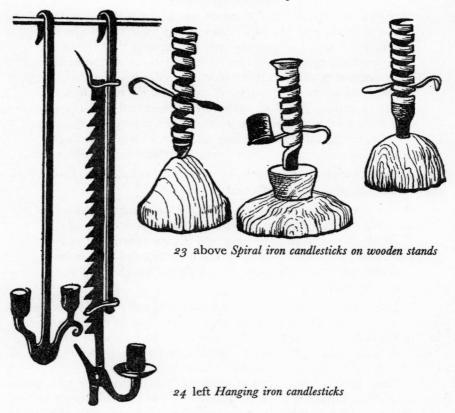

23 above *Spiral iron candlesticks on wooden stands*

24 left *Hanging iron candlesticks*

Quantities of Castile soap were imported from Spain, until the wars stopped all trade between the two countries. London soap boilers made three kinds—speckled, which was the most expensive, white, and grey, which was the cheapest. These were sold by the firkin and people added their own perfumes.

Babies were tightly swaddled and only rarely bathed. When this became necessary, great care was taken to protect the child from cold. Scented sheets, fresh from a hot press, were hung about the room to keep out draughts. To make the wooden tub more comfortable, sponges were arranged inside for the baby to lean against and sit on. He was rinsed in fresh, warm, scented water before being put to bed.

A newborn baby's first drink was traditionally a sip of water in which a red-hot cinder had been dropped—presumably as a purifier. The first actual food given after weaning was a 'pap' of fine flour mixed with water, served in a 'pap-boat' which looked like a present-day gravy-boat. Wealthy mothers had them made of silver or pewter; in poor homes they were of earthenware.

Countrywomen were able to keep their homes relatively warm with wood gathered locally and, in many districts, with charcoal. In London, however, poor families suffered a great deal, owing to the increase in the price of 'sea cole'—so called because it came south by boat from open-cast pits in Northumberland and Durham. In 1595 the Privy Council wrote to the Bishop of Durham:

The prices of sea coles are of late risen to very high rates
within the city of London, to the great oppression of the poorer
sorts of people, who do use the same for their chiefest fuel. . . .

Timber was becoming scarce, too, for so much of it had been used recklessly for centuries, for houses, furniture, wagons and ships as well as for fuel.

A Dutch doctor, on a visit in 1560, wrote praising the state of rooms in the houses he visited in England:

The neate cleanliness, the exquisite fineness, the pleasaunte
and delightfull furniture in every poynte for household, wonder-
fully rejoysed; their chambers and parlours strawed over with
sweet herbes refreshed me; their nosegayes finely entermingled
wyth sundry sortes of fragrante floures in their bedchambers
and privy rooms, with a comfortable smell cheered mee up
and entirelye delighted all my sences. . . .

Dr Andrew Boorde, that witty, wise and much-travelled physician, also wrote a great deal and gave much sound and human advice on all manner of subjects. His comment on housework seems to be tinged with more than a little interest in masculine comfort:

Swepynge of howses and chambres ought not to be done as
long as any honest man is within the precynts of the howse,
for the dust doth putryfy the ayre making it dence.

25 Sixteenth-century laundry

7

The Seventeenth Century

THE discovery of the New World set new problems in the English kitchen. For centuries house-wives had been experienced in drying, salting and smoking meat for winter use, but now other foods had to be provided in palatable form for longer voyages than sailors or merchants had ever before undertaken.

It was from Plymouth, Bristol and other western ports that people set sail across the Atlantic, and it was inevitably in the West Country that recipes for preserving foods proliferated in the sixteenth and seventeenth centuries. Hams were smoked, cream was baked, sweetened and bottled in Somerset, Devon and Cornwall and it is still in those counties that we buy it similarly 'clotted'.

The dread of sailors on long voyages was the 'unaccountable' disease called scurvy. In 1579 William Hakluyt had written:

> By reason of navigation, the sailors fall with sundry diseases;
> their gummes waxe great and swell, and all the body becometh
> sore, and so benummed that they cannot stirre hand or foot.

Thousands of men died before any hint of a cause was discovered. Vitamins were, of course, unknown, but gradually it was realized that fresh fruit provided both a preventative and a gradual cure. West Country orchards provided the fruits for the outward voyages and West Country housewives the skill in preserving other foods suitable for life at sea.

Until the discovery of the New World, all luxury imports had come to English kitchens from the Spice Islands of the East, and exotic eastern recipes had come with them. Now, new and untried materials were brought from the West—potatoes, sugars, treacle, chocolate, coffee and various new fruits, all came to seventeenth-century European kitchens from 'plantations' in the New World—mainly, at first, from the West Indies.

Francis Bacon, in his essay *Of Plantations,* wrote of the success of the colonists in Virginia after 1607, and advised about the kind of people who would make the best colonists, and about the kitchen requirements in a new country:

> The people wherewith you plant ought to be gardeners,
> ploughmen, labourers, smiths, carpenters, joiners, fishermen,
> fowlers, with some few apothecaries, surgeons, cooks, and
> bakers. In a country of plantation, first look about what kind
> of victual the country yields of itself to hand . . . then consider
> what victual or esculent things there are which grow speedily.
> Above all, there ought to be brought store of biscuit, oatmeal,
> flour, meal and the like, in the beginning till bread be made.

The adventurers who sailed three thousand miles west from England to establish a new society built their homes of whatever materials they could find, and in a style as much like their earlier homes as they could manage. Pioneer wives, struggling to raise families in the wilderness, gritted their teeth, rolled up their sleeves, and probably cooked everything from buffalo tongue to beaver tail. Once settled on farms and plantations, with an increasing variety of foods at hand, they were busy from dawn to dusk and bought nothing that could be raised, grown or cooked at home.

However varied in background they were, the discipline of the wilderness soon brought them to a democratic level. The gentleman felled the wood for his log cabin side by side with the ploughman; and mistress and maid, living in the log cabin together, became companions and shared the domestic work. The class of persons who were called 'servants' in England, were called 'helps' in America.

These early colonists took with them English grain for immediate sowing and large numbers of swine. In England mutton was popular, as a result of the importance of the wool industry and its need for enormous numbers of sheep. In the colonies the wild briars that covered so much of the wilderness damaged the fleeces of grazing sheep and discouraged farmers from raising them in any quantity. Virginians therefore preferred venison to mutton, and modern Americans still import most of the mutton they eat.

In colonial Virginia basement kitchens were at first very common. As the colonists grew more prosperous, homes of course became more comfortable and the kitchen was often built as a separate building, behind the main house, so that the family could be spared smells and excessive heat. It was often a one-room structure with a large open fireplace and a dresser displaying whatever pewter and earthenware they had been able to bring with them. The seats were simple stools or benches; trenchers were made of wood, and were often spoken of as having 'the dinner side' and 'the pie side'. Two people often ate from the same dish; if a couple shared a trencher it was considered that they were betrothed.

In a large plantation house the kitchen was usually the largest room, except for the ballroom. It sometimes had a loft above, used for dry storage or as a bedroom for the kitchen servants. In the southern colonies the kitchen ceiling was always high and the windows tall, because of the intense heat. For cross-ventilation in hot weather there were windows on each wall except the chimney one.

Refrigeration and canning were of course not yet dreamed of, so the colonial housewife had to depend upon other expedients to keep her food supplies fresh. Salt meat was served regularly, but getting salt was a continual problem, since the waters of Chesapeake Bay were of low salinity. Different qualities of salt were used for different purposes: common, or 'Liverpool' salt was for table use, but superior 'bay' salt, from the Bay of Biscay, was needed for curing meat or fish. When they could not get salt, some women followed the Indian method and dried their meat by very slow cooking out of doors.

Southern planters entertained lavishly, for towns were a long way apart, there was plenty of home-grown produce and servants were easy to find. Wealthy Virginian families breakfasted between eight and nine o'clock of bread, butter, venison, ham, beef, and tea or coffee. They dined in the middle of the day and had a light supper at eight or nine at night. Modest families ate cold turkey—a local bird, easily snared—and fried hominy with cider for breakfast, pork with (sweet) corn and cabbage at midday, and usually they had no supper. The food must often have been tepid and limp, since it was prepared in an outside kitchen, but it was lavish and highly seasoned.

The mistress of a colonial plantation house may have done little actual housework herself, but she took pains to oversee every detail of the servants' work in the household. On her wrist she carried a little key basket, filled with keys which unlocked the wine cellar, the store cupboards, the smoke-house, the linen press, and her own desk and sewing table. She might personally wash the glass and silverware and—in the eighteenth century—the new china tea-sets; she nursed the sick, taught her children to read perhaps, and embroidered endless cushions, cloths and hangings for the house. The wives of less wealthy men had an enormous amount of cooking, salting, drying and distilling to do, and had to be able to handle a gun in case of attack. They were, literally, living on the fringe of civilization.

In spite of religious and political troubles, the seventeenth century was a prosperous time in England. The new colonies gave wealth and power to merchants, to the noblemen who were sent to administer the new settlements, and to English society as a whole. It was a time of lavish, warm-hearted enjoyment of civilized living and much of the new wealth was spent on houses and gardens and on entertaining. Dining tables reflected general prosperity. Samuel Pepys was not alone in trying to improve the appearance of his table. On September 9th 1664 he went 'out and bought some things; among others, a dozen of silver salts'. In the same year he 'payed the silver-smith £22.18s for spoons, forks, and sugar-box'. In 1666 he bought 'drinking glasses, a case of knives and other things' and evidently felt by the end of that year that he had 'arrived', for he wrote:

> One thing I reckon remarkable in my own condition is, that
> I am come to abound in good plate so as at all entertainments
> to be served wholly with silver plates, having two dozen
> and a half.

26 right *Knife box*
27 left *Salt box*

So we can visualize the seventeenth-century kitchen, in 'middling' homes as well as grand ones, as being busy and exciting and more competitive than that of earlier times. Servants shared their employers' pride in rising standards.

A farmer's wife led a very busy and varied life, as always. According to an early seventeenth-century writer:

> They have the charge of the oven and the cellar; and we
> leave the handling of hemp to them likewise; as also the care
> of making webs, of looking to the clipping of sheep, of keeping
> their fleeces, of spinning and combing the wool to make cloth
> to clothe the family; of ordering the kitchen garden; and keeping

of the fruits, herbs, roots and seeds; and moreover of watching and tending to the bees.

Dyeing is not mentioned in that list, but it was an important household responsibility. Vegetable dyes were made from berries, lichens, bark, roots and leaves; goose grease was saved for oiling the wool after it was washed; and finally that new labour-saving device, the spinning wheel, was in virtually continual use by both the mistress and her maidservants.

Butter was made at home, in the dairy of a large house and in the kitchen of a smaller one. A variety of wooden utensils had to be scrubbed and boiled before and after use: ladles, skimmers, milk-pans, butter-pots, salting-troughs, scales and tubs. If cheese was made there would be a cheese-press, sometimes in a separate cheese-room fitted with racks on which the cheeses were laid to mature.

For her dairy-work the housewife had to have a cool hand for butter and a strong arm for cheese. Thomas Tusser, in his *Good Pointes,* made it clear that dairy-work must be carefully supervised:

Ill housewife unskilful to make her own cheese
through trusting to others, hath this for her fees:
Her milkpans and cream pots so clabber'd and sost
that butter is wanting and cheese is half lost.

The gradual replacement of wood by coal for domestic use meant, of course, a change in the fireplace, for it was impossible to kindle coal on a flat hearth. Andirons were unsuitable for use with 'sea coles' and were replaced in up-to-date households by various types of brazier or fire-basket raised above the hearth to allow an up-draught. In 1635 a certain John Sibthorpe took out a patent for an oven which could 'be used with sea coles or any other coles digged out of the earth, and therewith may bake as soone and as fayre and for less charge than they now doe in heating with wood'. The innovation was expensive and used only in wealthy households at first. The open hearth remained in most families for another two hundred years.

This was a time of great contrasts in Britain and there were thousands of families living in terrible poverty, like the weaver of Hastings, with whom the poet John Taylor found lodging in 1623:

No meat, no drink, no lodging (but the floor)
No stool to sit, no lock upon the door,
No straw to make us litter in the night,
Nor any candlestick to hold the light.

Habits of eating and drinking were becoming virtually universal throughout Europe. Forks were mentioned in Italian cookery books in the sixteenth century, but they only slowly took on in England, because of the traditional English suspicion of all habits introduced from abroad.

With the Restoration of Charles II to the throne in 1660 habits changed markedly. Charles and his entourage had lived in France and in Holland throughout the Cromwellian period, and continental ideas became fashionable in England once the new Court was established.

New table implements began to appear—knives with rounded, instead of pointed ends, spoons with egg-shaped bowls and flat stems, in place of the fig-shaped bowl and rounded stem of earlier days.

It was Thomas Coryat, an eccentric English traveller, who introduced the idea of a new table implement and his comments suggest that English habits were still insanitary:

> The Italians do always at their meals use a little fork when
> they cut their meat. This form of feeding I understand is
> generally used in all places in Italy, their forks being for the
> most part made of iron or steel and some of silver, but those
> are used only by gentlemen. The reason of their curious custom
> is because the Italian cannot by any means endure to have
> his dish touched with fingers, seeing all men's fingers are
> not alike clean. Hereupon I myself thought good to imitate the
> Italian fashion by this forked cutting of meat.

It was the special pride of the good housewife or cook to keep the spits as bright as the table cutlery, for they too came into contact with the food impaled on them. For grand banquets, spits of silver were sometimes used, and the food carried to the table on them.

Many housewives made collections of their recipes and ways of housekeeping. The quantity and variety of materials used and the time taken give us an insight into the busy, creative life led by women in pre-industrial days. In 1684 a Mrs Hannah Woolley published *The Queen-like Closet*:

> To make misers for Children to eat in Afternoons in Summer:
> Take half a pint of good small beer, two spoonfuls of Sack,
> the Crum of half a penny Manchet, two handfuls of Currans
> washed clean and dried, and a little of grated-Nutmeg, and a
> little Sugar, so give it to them cold.

> To Candy Flowers: Boil some Rosewater and Sugar together,
> then put in your Flowers, being very dry, and boil them a
> little, then strew in some fine Sugar over them, and turn them,
> and boil them a little more, and take them from the fire, and
> strew some more Sugar over them, then take them out and

lay them to dry, and open them and strew Sugar over them; they will dry in a few hours in a hot day.

To perfume Gloves: Take four Grains of Musk and grind it with Rosewater, and also eight grains of Civet, then take two spoonfuls of Gum-dragon steeped all night in Rosewater, beat these to a thin jelly, putting in a half a spoonful of Oil of Cloves, Cinnamon and Jessamine mixed together, then take a Spunge and dip it therein, and rub the Gloves all over thin, lay them in a dry clean place eight and fourty hours, then rub them with your hand till they become limber.

Salads were eaten a great deal, and John Evelyn the diarist gave detailed directions for their preparation:

A sallat [should contain] crude and fresh herbs to be eaten with some acetous juice, oil, salt, etc. to give them a grateful gust and vehicle.

These 'herbs' must be washed and shaken in a cloth, and cut with a silver knife, not a steel one. Then 'all should fall into their places like the notes in music, in which there should be nothing harsh or grating'. Garlic, he says 'is not for ladies' palates nor those who court them'.

The Clerk of the Kitchen at Woburn Abbey kept a 'Kitchen-Book' which was signed by the Earl of Bedford every week. This book recorded all expenses for food for the household and for visitors; there was also a petty cash book in which were recorded such items as mops, brushes, cleaning materials, and the many yards of coarse cloth used for making bags and dusters. The Clerk needed, too, a small amount of cash in hand to reward messengers who brought goods to the house, and to pay the pedlars who supplied such articles as thread, needles and tape, for the use of the maids. All these details had to be approved by the Earl's signature.

By the end of the century ladies were learning to keep accounts as well as inventories and recipes. A notable example was set by Lady Grisell Baillie, whose wonderful household books, with their minute accounts of all expenditure, were published by the Scottish History Society early in this century.

Lady Grisell paid:

	£	s.	d.
For a pound of white pepper		3	6
For 8 lb. Barlie at 3d. per lb.		2	0
For a litle botle of Hungary Water			
[a famous cure for rheumatism]		1	3
For a lb. Bohea Tea		16	0

For a lb Beco Tea	1	4	0
For ¼lb fine green Tea		8	0

A tax on soap and candles had been imposed and was bitterly resented, so Lady Grisell had to pay 5/– for two lb of wax candles, and 'For a firriken of sope brick this day £1.8s.' 'Sope' for two weeks cost her 5/– and soap and sand to scour the house was 3/–. Samuel Pepys referred to lighting by candles on December 15th 1684:

This night I begun to burn wax candles in my closet at the office, to try the charge, and to see whether the smoke offends like that of tallow candles.

Paper was still relatively expensive and bills were often made out on one sheet and receipted by the various tradesmen in their different handwritings. For example, on the back of an unreceipted bill:

	£	s.	d.
For 3 large saucepans		13	6
One stew pann		10	0

... there are a number of small bills and receipts, such as:

'Rec^ed then of ye Lady Osbaldeston ye sum of four pounds for 8 wallnutt mattd chairs and all commands   By Mr Jno Davis.'

and

'Recd febear 10. 1709
Of the Lady Osbaldeston for a par of
Drors £2.5.0 by mee George Gordon.'

Laundry was normally a monthly or three-monthly occurrence in a large house, and must have been a time of excitement and jollification. Some people did a great wash, called a 'bucking' only twice a year. Washerwomen were employed to help the servants if necessary, but in a more modest home, such as that of Mr and Mrs Samuel Pepys, the mistress and her maid tackled it together. At one o'clock on a frosty morning in January, Mr Pepys went to bed and left his wife and the maid 'a-washing still', and on another occasion he wrote: 'Home, and being washing day, dined upon cold meat.' Domestic customs change remarkably little in hundreds of years!

Near the laundry there was, in many households, an enclosed drying-ground where the clothes were hung out to dry on lines, or spread over sweet-smelling bushes in fine weather.

Mrs Bruce, housekeeper to the Earl of Bedford, employed a number of anonymous 'women who came in to clean', before the annual migration of the Earl's family to their London home, Bedford

House, in the Strand. As well as scouring the pewter, washing the floors and 'cleaning the irons', we see from the bills which were made out at Mrs Bruce's dictation—she evidently could not write—reference to such laundry items as:

July 1675   For washing sheets and napkins before the
            great wash when the two masters was in town 2s. 0d.
            For three women one day to wash   4s. 6d.
            For washing of twelve pair of sheets
            at 4d per pair   4s. 0d.

And another item which confirms that human behaviour has changed very little in three hundred years:

A woman six days to help to wash all the rooms after
the workmen left the house   6s. 0d.

Soap was made at home from a mixture of tallow, olive oil and ashes dissolved in water. Women exchanged recipes just as they did for preserves. We read of various kinds of soap—Crowne, Joppa, Bristol, Irish, Windsor, Genoa, Black, Green and Liquid. One recipe was for 'eighteen bushels of ashes, one bushel of stone lime, three pounds of tallow, fifteen pounds of the purest Barbary wax of a lovely green colour, and a peck of salt'.

Sir Hugh Platt, in *Delightes for Ladies*, recommended 'a delicate washing ball' perfumed with rose-leaves, lavender flowers, orris root, cypress and scrapings of Castille soap. For 'a ball to take out stains from linen' he recommended hard white soap, sliced lemons and roche allum, rolled into a ball and rubbed on the dirty mark. Stained hands could best be cleaned with the juice of sorrel.

At Haddon Hall, Derbyshire, there is a wooden washing 'tally', measuring $5\frac{1}{2}$ inches by $4\frac{1}{2}$ inches, with fifteen squares drawn on it, each marked with the name of a piece of clothing. The whole board is covered with a piece of horn held in place by strips of brass nailed with ornamental brass nails. Under each name is a movable dial, numbered 0–12, very much like the indicators we put out for the milkman nowadays (See picture 23.)

Mangles were rare and in most households washing had to be wrung out by hand. Ironing was a laborious business. There were flat-irons which had to be stood on a trivet by the fire; box-irons which had to have a hot brick or piece of iron, or hot charcoal, inside; and goffering irons, heated in a similar way, for crimping ruffs and lace frills.

A supply of fresh water was a problem in many areas and in some seasons. It was a serious offence to make an unofficial connection with any public pipes provided, and the cleanliness of public water

28 Chimney iron and box-irons

taps was a frequent concern of the manorial courts. The manor court at Petworth, in Sussex, fined a woman two pence for washing bullocks' entrails at one of the taps, and watering horses and washing fish there were other offences. Thought was being given to improving supplies in many towns. A Frenchman, travelling in England at the beginning of the century, wrote of drinking water in London being enclosed in stone cisterns and 'let off through cocks into special wooden iron-bound vessels with broad bottoms and narrow tops, which poor labourers carry to and from the houses on their shoulders and sell'.

But by the middle of the century supplies had improved, as this verse of 1644 shows:

Some ten years since, fresh water there was scant,
But with much cost they have supplied the want.
By a most exc'lent water-work that's made,
And to th' Town in Pipes it is conveyed,

So that each man of note there always can
But turne a Cock within his house, and still
They have freshwater always at their will,
This have they all, unto their great content,
For which they each do pay a yearly rent.

The Pepys household certainly had running water, for the amiable diarist wrote that Jane, one of their chain of many maids, washed his feet in herb-scented water before putting him to bed.

29 Goffering iron, for crimping a ruff

However, this service did not prevent him from beating her with a broom on occasions when she was not tidy enough about the house!

On another occasion Pepys was evidently ashamed of his rough treatment of a servant, for in February 1665 he wrote:

> Coming home, saw my door and hatch open, left so by Luce our cookmaid, which so vexed me, that I did give her a kick in our entry, and offered a blow at her, and was seen doing so by Sir W. Pen's footboy, which did vex me to the heart, because I know he will be telling their family of it.

We learn a good deal of what professional people ate from Pepys's diary. The diarist evidently delighted in his meals:

> Very merry we were with our pasty very well baked; and a good dish of roasted chickens, pease, lobsters, strawberries.

> Home, having brought with me from Fenchurch Street a hundred of sparrow grass, cost 18d. We had them and a little bit of salmon—cost 3s.

> Dined at home in the garret, where my wife dressed the remains of a turkey, and in the doing of it she burnt her hand.

Coffee gradually became known in England after the middle of the century and by 1690 it was available in comparatively large quantities. From 1670 the Earl of Bedford's accounts at Woburn Abbey record the occasional purchase of very small quantities of coffee for

1 Neolithic stone house at Skara Brae, Orkney, 1500 BC. All the furniture is of stone. *(Crown Copyright: reproduced by permission of the Department of the Environment)*
2 Bronze tankard from Trawsfynydd, Merionethshire, Wales. *(City of Liverpool Museum)*

3 Wall painting of a Roman country villa, AD 300. *(Landesmuseum, Trier)*
4 Mosaic floor of the dining-room at Chedworth Roman villa, Glos. *(National Monuments Record. Crown Copyright)*

5

6

5 A family meal, from a Roman tombstone in Yorkshire. *(The Yorkshire Museum)*
6 A section of the Bayeux tapestry, showing soldiers cooking out of doors, serving
   meat on small spits, and feasting. *(Reading Museum and Art Gallery)*

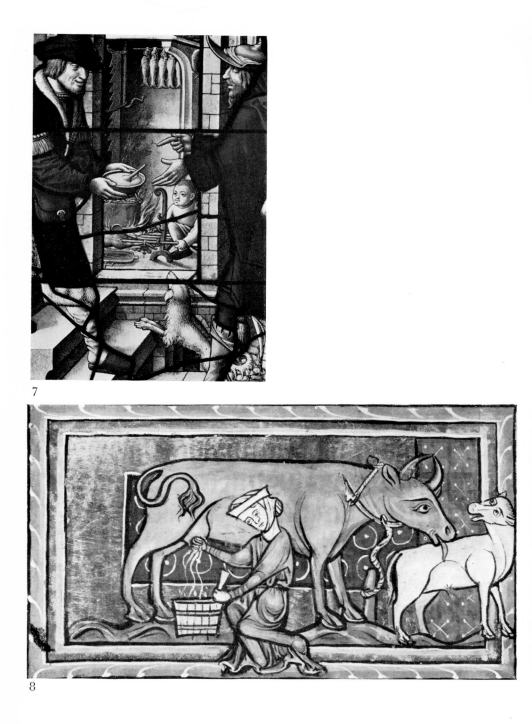

7 Part of a stained-glass window, showing an early medieval turnspit roasting a bird and smoking fish. (*Victoria and Albert Museum*)

8 A dairymaid, from a medieval bestiary, or treatise on animals. (*The Curators of the Bodleian Library, Oxford*)

9

10

11

12

9 The abbot's kitchen, Glastonbury Abbey. Early fifteenth century. Inside is a fine
vaulted roof and four large fireplaces. *(By kind permission of the Trustees)*

10 Cooking husband's supper, from a fifteenth-century manuscript. *(British Museum)*

11 A royal feast, from a fifteenth-century manuscript. Notice the elaborate hangings,
but plain furniture and sparse table. *(British Museum)*

12 A peasant home, from a fifteenth-century manuscript. *(British Museum)*

13

14

13 A glass roundel showing a middle-class dining table. Early sixteenth century.
   Notice the salt box, bellows and napkins. *(Victoria and Albert Museum)*
14 Washday in 1582. *(British Museum)*

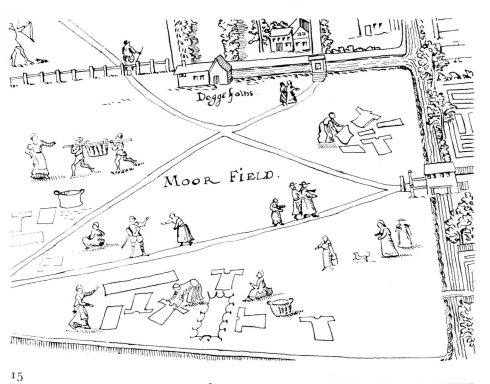

Dogge halns

MOOR FIELD.

15

16

17

15 Laundresses at work in Moorfields, from a sixteenth-century map of London.
    (The London Museum)
16 Buying eggs in the market, from the 1495 translation of a book by Bartholomaeus
    Anglicus. *(B. T. Batsford Ltd)*
17 The Water Bearer. *(The Curators of the Bodleian Library, Oxford)*

18

18 *The Idle Servant* by Nicolaes Maes, 1636–93. *(Reproduced by courtesy of the Trustees, The National Gallery, London)*

19

20

19 A woman and her servant. From a painting by Emanuel de Witte, 1617–92. (*Rijksmuseum, Amsterdam*)

20 *Peasant family at Meal-time* by Jan Steen, 1625–79. (*Reproduced by courtesy of the Trustees, The National Gallery, London*)

21

21 A poor home, from the painting by Adriaen van Ostade, 1610–85. *(Museum Boymans-van Beuningen, Rotterdam)*

22

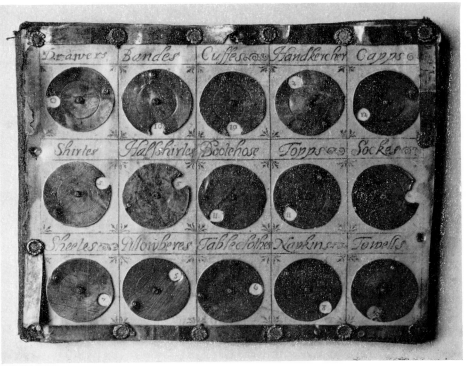

23

22 *The Linen Cupboard* by Pieter de Hooch, 1629–84. *(Rijksmuseum, Amsterdam)*
23 Washing tally of beechwood covered with horn. *(Haddon Hall Museum, by kind permission of His Grace the Duke of Rutland)*

24

24 The Wolsey Kitchen, Hampton Court Palace. *(Crown Copyright)*

25

26

25 Cheese-making in the dairy, 1699. *(B. T. Batsford Ltd)*
26 A wealthy family taking tea, 1720. Notice the different ways of holding the
porcelain cups without handles. *(Victoria and Albert Museum)*

27 *Saying Grace* by Joseph van Aken. *(Ashmolean Museum, Oxford)*

28

29

28 English delftware tray, 1743. An Indian servant waits on the family at tea.
  (*Victoria and Albert Museum*)
29 *Plucking the Turkey* by Henry Walton, 1746–1813. (*The Tate Gallery, London*)

30

31

30 *Kitchen at Newcastle Emlyn*, by Thomas Rowlandson 1756–1827. *(British Museum. Photograph: Harriet Bridgeman Ltd)*
31 Welsh dresser. *(The National Museum of Wales, Welsh Folk Museum)*

32 A farm kitchen in Northumberland, 1778. *(British Museum)*
33 Dancing in the servants' hall. *(British Museum)*

34

35

34 Cottage industry in the kitchen 1791. Engraving from a painting by W. Hincks.
   (British Museum. Photograph: Harriet Bridgeman Ltd)
35 Drama in the kitchen! *c.* 1820. *(Radio Times Hulton Picture Library)*

36

37

36 A well-ordered kitchen in a wealthy eighteenth-century house.
37 Great Kitchen of the Royal Pavilion, Brighton. (*The Royal Pavilion, Brighton*)

THE NEW DOMESTIC COOKERY.

38

39

38 From a cookery book of about 1830. *(Radio Times Hulton Picture Library)*
39 His kitchen in London in 1846, drawn by Sir George Scharf. *(Radio Times Hulton Picture Library)*

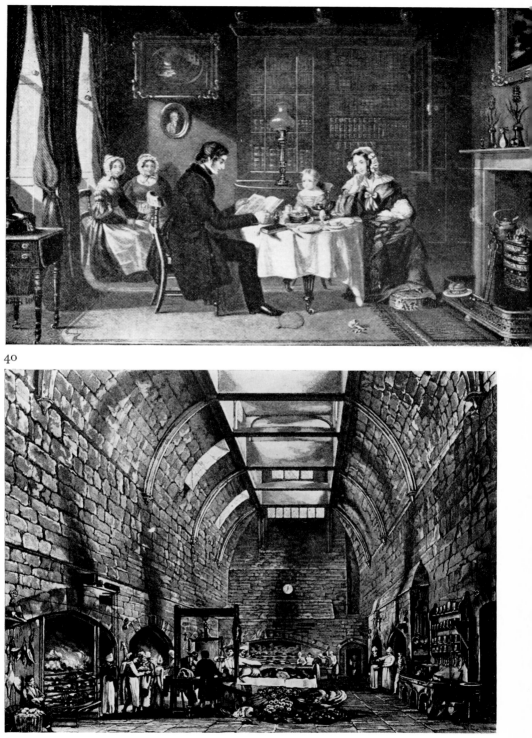

40 A Victorian breakfast, with maids in attendance.
41 The Great Kitchen, Windsor Castle, 1818. *(Radio Times Hulton Picture Library)*

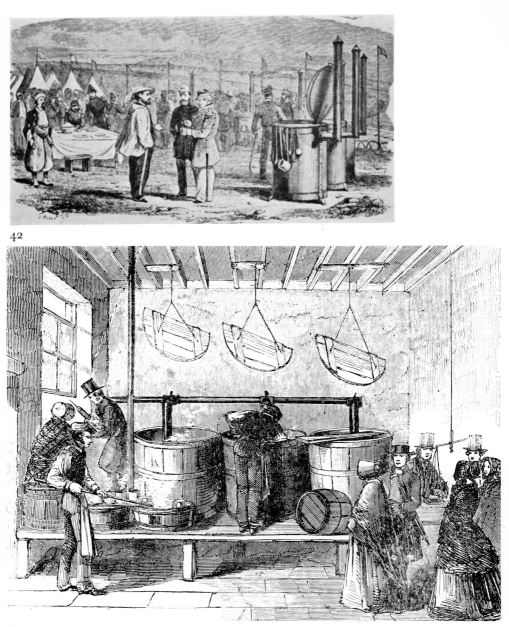

42

43

42 Soyer's camp kitchen in the Crimea.
43 A Society of Friends' soup kitchen during the Irish famine of 1847. *(Radio Times Hulton Picture Library)*

44

45

44 Roasting fifty-six geese on a spit for the inmates of the Old Men's Hospital,
   Norwich. Late nineteenth century. *(Radio Times Hulton Picture Library)*
45 Mrs Beeton *(The National Portrait Gallery, London)*

46

47

48

46 The Leamington stove, or kitchener, illustrated in Mrs Beeton's *Book of Household Management*, 1861.
47 American 'dual-purpose' stove of the eighteen-sixties.
48 Title page of American cookery book published in Philadelphia, 1844.

49

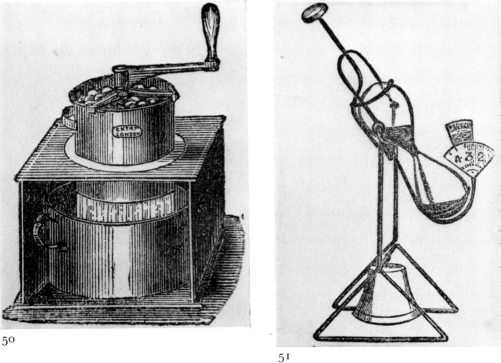

50

51

49 Nineteenth-century American 'dual-purpose' stove with hot water tank attached.
 (*Radio Times Hulton Picture Library*)
50 Rotary masher for vegetables, manufactured by the George Kent Company in 1879.
51 Signal egg-boiler. An ingenious device on the market in 1879. Sand in a glass
 was so adjusted that when the sand ran out, the glass tilted and rang a bell.

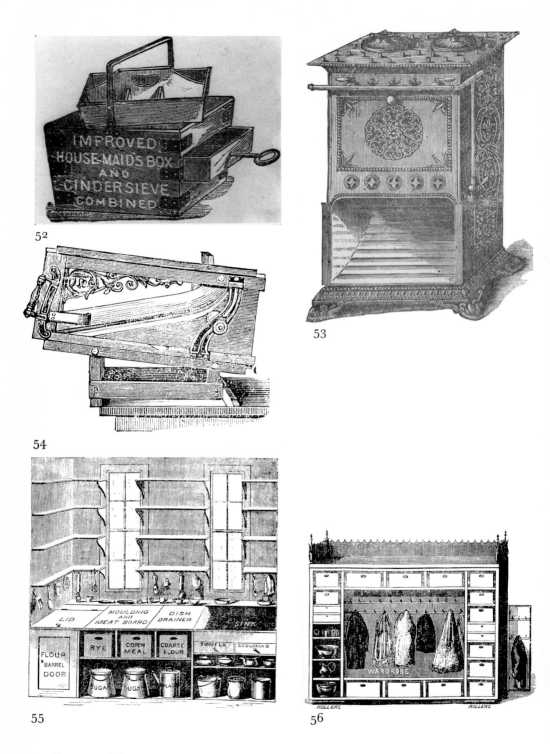

52 'Improved' housemaid's box, 1879.
53 Introduced from France, this combined heating and cooking stove of 1879 could be used for roasting, baking, boiling and grilling simultaneously.
54 Bread-cutting machine, 1879. Manufactured by Messrs Summerscales of Keighley, Yorkshire, this machine could cut bread to any degree of thickness.
55 and 56 Well-planned sink unit and fitted wardrobe, as suggested by Catherine Beecher in *The American Woman's Home*, published in 1869.

57

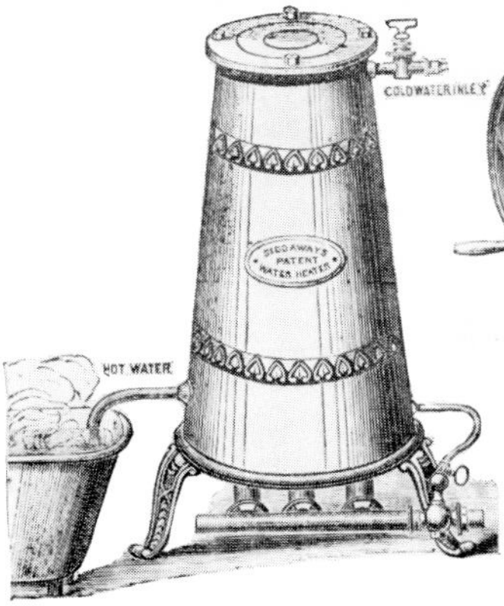

COLD WATER INLET
SIDDAWAYS PATENT WATER HEATER
HOT WATER

58

59

• A·LYSTE •
• OF · YE · FARE •
• PROVYDED · FOR · YE · OWLES · & · FOWLS ·
• Ye · Cockie · Leekie · Soupe · Soupe mayd from ye Hare · and ye foreiggn kynd yclept Julliene . . .
• Turbot Fyshe wyth ye sauce of Lobsters ·
• Ye great Codde · serued wyth Oysters Sauce ·
· Ye noble Sir Loin of Beefe · wyth · Puddynge of Yorke · Ye rygghte royale : Saddle of Mutton · sweete jellie serued therewyth · Pickled Beefe
Turkie boyled · wyth Maccaroni in ye Italiane fashionne · Yorkeshire Ham
· Victoria Puddynge · Ye rygghte glorious Plum Puddynge · Apples curiouslie cookyd · Prunes and Jellies
NM

60

THE SERVANT'S FRIEND
SPONG & Co
PATENTEES LONDON
PATENT KNIFE CLEANER

61

57 Orange-peel cutter. Another invention of the Kent Company, this machine, although small, could slice all vegetables to any required size.
58 Siddaways patent water-heater, 1880.
59 'Paragon' washing machine of 1880.
60 A quaint menu of the eighteen-eighties.
61 'The Servant's Friend' knife-cleaner, 1880. The following announcement appeared in an advertisement of the time: ' "The Servant's Friend" does not belie its name, quickly imparting a lustrous polish to knives.'

62

63

62 Kitchen of Royal Holloway College, Egham. *(Radio Times Hulton Picture Library)*
63 'Excelsior' refrigerators, 1885. *Left:* made of grained oak and specially designed with two separate compartments for cooling wine; *right:* pine-grained with three compartments.

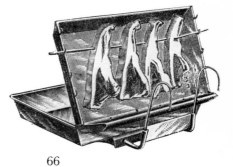

66

67

68

64 One of the first stoves manufactured from aluminium, 1900.
65 Nineteenth-century pressure or 'steam' cooker.
66 The 'patent frizzler' of 1898 combined an adaptation of the spit with an improvement on the principle of the Dutch oven.
67 'Thompson's patent teapot', 1885.
68 An advertisement for baking powder appearing in 1886.

70

71

69 Advertisement for soap appearing in the *Graphic* in 1908. *(Radio Times Hulton Picture Library)*
70 A Yorkshire farmhouse kitchen still in use today.
71 An early Edwardian kitchen.

72 The kitchen of today: easy and pleasant to work in. *(Wrighton International Furniture Ltd)*

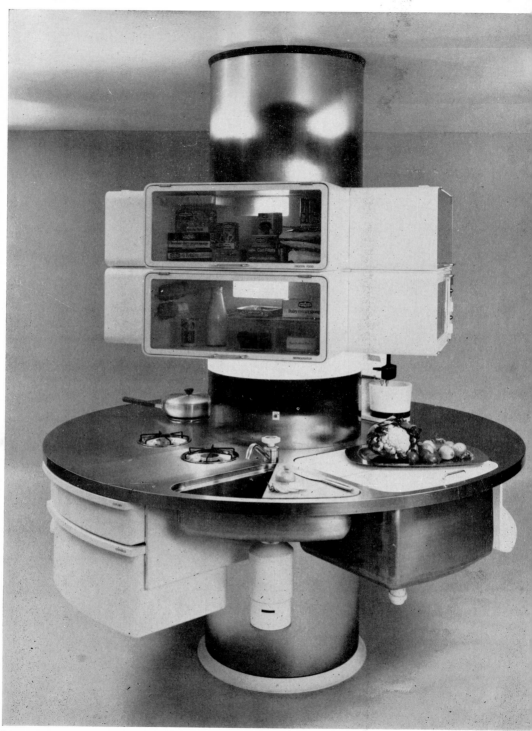

73

73 The kitchen of tomorrow? A single cylindrical unit with grouped cooking and storage facilities in two tiers which revolve independently round a central service core. Designed by Ilana Henderson. *(The Council of Industrial Design)*

the personal use of himself and the Countess. In 1670, too, there is mention of the purchase of a coffee-pot, a china dish and nine shillings' worth of coffee; during the next year a set was bought for the Countess. From 1685 one pound of coffee powder appears as a regular item in the grocery bill, for the general use of the household. Chocolate was less popular at first, but was drunk increasingly during the eighteenth century.

Special pots and cups were used for coffee, as for tea, and each person in a well-to-do family had his own equipment. Middle-class families could not afford to drink either tea or coffee at first, but in spite of dire warnings from physicians and moralists, the habit gradually spread.

The practice of spicing wine was still in vogue. For generations, the most popular spiced wine was Hippocras, which was made from wine and sugar or honey, cinnamon, ginger and pepper, and then strained. Pepys recorded that he was offered some, 'it being, to the best of my present judgement, only a mixed compound drink, and not any wine'. But he was mistaken, for it was very potent!

The still-room was used for making cosmetics as well as wines. Eggs and asses' milk were much used, and almost every flower and herb in cultivation. Hair was dyed gold with rhubarb infused in white wine, or with honey mixed with gum arabic, and dyed red with radish and privet.

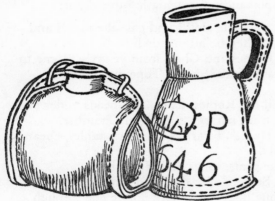

30 Leather bottle and blackjack

The nature of household service was changing rapidly at this time. Even grand households no longer employed the sons of gentlemen to the extent which had been normal hitherto. In *The Compleat Serving Maid*, published in 1677, are listed many functions which could not be carried out by 'young maidens'—we read for the first time of chamber-maids, cook-maids, under-cook-maids, nursery-maids, dairy-maids, laundry-maids, house-maids and scullery-maids. The sons of gentlemen, and others who might formerly have worked as stewards or chamberlains or gentlemen ushers in the service of a wealthy household, now went into business or into one of the professions. Possibilities were expanding for everyone.

31 Cast-iron fire-dogs and fire-back

The directions for maid-servants in *The Compleat Serving Maid* are given in tabular form for every day of the week, for the author believed strongly in the importance of systematic supervision:

Mondays—Looke out the foule cloths and cale the maids and sit and stay by them till they be all mended.
Tuesdays—Clene the Romes and Chers from ye great Rome to the norsery and ye beads [beds?] on ye Tope and botum, and dust ye feathers.
Wednesdays—Clene all the Romes, Chers and beads onder and Tope with ye feathers from norsery to ye Egal Chamber.
Thursdays—Clene ye Hall and Parlors windows, tables, chears, and Pictors below stairs.
Fridays—Scoure all the grats, tongs and Hand-Irons.
Saturdays—Clene the Store House shelf and Dressers.
Everyday—Once for one houre in ye fore noune goe through all ye Romes and see it doith not Raine into them and dust them all doune and swipe them.

The cook's duties were as follows:

Cooke-maid—Washe yor chitchen every night, and the Larders every other day—Shelfes and dressers, and scoure the puter we use every Friday night, and all the Rest of ye puter once every month. Kepe yor chitchen exthridubary clene. To helpe upon washing dayes the Rest of ye maids to wash. And make all ye maids bring doune there candellstickes ye first thinge in a morning to be maid clene.

Lady Grisell Baillie seems to have been a delightful woman, but she had many staffing problems in her Scottish home. During ten years sixty different names appear in her account books, of which thirty-one stayed for less than a year! Of ten different cooks engaged in one year, one remained for only a day, another for one night, and a third for two months, but was then taken away by the constables. The very strict instructions Lady Baillie gave to her housekeeper go a long way to explain why she could not keep her staff:

To get up airly is most necessary to see that all the maids and other servants be about their proper business. . . . The dayry carefully lookt after, you to keep the kie of the inner milk house where the butter and milk is. . . . Keep the maids close at their spining till 9 at night when they are not washing or at other necessary work, weigh out to them exactly the soap, and often go to the wash house to see it is not wasted but made the proper use of, and that there be no linnen washt there but those of the family that are alowed to do it . . . get account

32 Chamber-maid

from the chamber maid of what candles she gets from you for
the rooms and see there be no waste of candle nor fire
any where. . . .

Wages were usually paid at the quarter, or the half-quarter, and
sometimes yearly. In the Howard 'Household Book' there is an entry:
'To James the Butler for one year due about Whitsunday 40/–'. A cook
in a large house received £4 a year in 1630 (an amount which Pepys,
a little later, grumbled at having to pay), a housemaid £3 and a dairymaid £3. Many of the women in the Earl of Bedford's household were
given clothes, both as part-salary and as presents. Many of the young
people who are mentioned in the accounts—'Tom-in-the-Kitchen' and
'Alice-about-the-house', for example—were paid no wages, but were
fed and given a bed and clothing.

8

The Eighteenth Century

THE 'offices' of a middling Georgian house consisted of kitchen, sculleries, pantries, chinaclosets and wash-house. In grander houses there were also a laundry, a still-room, a buttery, a bakehouse, a dairy and a brewery. These quarters were all situated as far away from the family's living rooms as possible, so as to make sure that neither smell nor noise could affect their comfort. Often the kitchen was a separate building connected with the main house by a covered passage, so food must often have come to table cold. In more modest homes, the kitchen was usually the main living room.

As well as producing its own food, a country household still had to make its own fuel and lights, its linen, clothes and medicines. There was no ready-cooked food to be had, except in London and a few other towns where a few pie-shops existed.

Every household still had to be largely self-sufficient, so a housewife in the eighteenth century still led a very busy life. Even if she had a large house and kept a great many servants, she would take pride in knowing precisely how every job should be done and in being quite as skilled as her maids. There were hams and sides of bacon to smoke, pickle or cure, fruits to bottle or dry or make into jams, and vegetables to pickle. Roses, violets, cowslips and other flowers were crystallized in sugar; herbs were grown and dried; butter had to be churned, cheese made, ale, cider, wine and mead to be brewed; and even soaps, perfumes and cosmetics were still made at home in many families.

When Mrs Lybbe Powys visited Holkham Hall, Norfolk, in 1756, she wrote in her diary:

> There are four wings; one contains all the offices in general,
> all answerable to the rest; such an amazing large and good

kitchen I never saw, everything in it so nice and clever. . . .
I've heard . . . Lady Leicester never misses going round this
wing every morning, and one day [I] was walking by the
windows, and saw her Ladyship in her kitchen at six o'clock,
thinking all her guests safe in bed, I suppose. Her dairy is the
neatest place you can imagine, the whole marble; in Norfolk
they never skim their cream off, as in other places, but let the
milk run from it . . . and the butter made into such pretty
patts hardly larger than a sixpence.

During the earlier part of the century, and later in old-fashioned
households, cooking was still done at a large, open fireplace or 'down-
hearth'. Coal was coming more and more into use, but many women
still preferred to cook with wood, of which birch was considered the
best. Some people found coal fires difficult to start, and the men who
delivered the 'coles' in towns often undertook fire-lighting as part of
their service.

The kitchen chimney was often cleaned by lighting a fire in it
and letting it burn itself out. But many people avoided this dangerous
practice by employing a sweep, and many sweeps employed small boys
to work for them. Charles Kingsley's *The Water Babies,* published in
1863, highlighted the plight of these wretched boys and must have been
the main topic of conversation in many kitchens throughout the country.

Charcoal was sometimes used for kitchen fires, but was thought
by many people to be unhealthy. Parson Woodforde, in *The Diary of a
Country Parson* noted that, when his niece Nancy was making jam, 'she
became giddy, too long at the stove where charcoal was burning,
though the outward door was open all the time'.

At the side of the kitchen fireplace there was usually an iron door
to a cupboard, in which dishes were kept hot and wine mulled, and in
which slow cooking could be done. The main baking was done in a
separate bread-oven, heated with brushwood. When the wood had
burnt away, the ashes were raked aside and a batch of loaves or cakes
put in. In some old houses a bulge can still be seen in the outside wall
which shows where the bread-oven used to be.

A remarkable portable kitchen was invented by Sir Samuel
Moreland and described by Roger North in his *Life of Lord Keeper
Guilford:*

He made a portable engine that moved by Watchwork, which
might be call'd a Kitchen, for it had a Fire-place and Grate,
with which he could make Soup, broil Costeletts, or roast an
Egg. . . . He said himself that this Machine cost him £30. He
took it with him in his own Coach and, at Innes, he was his
own Cook.

Many of the wealthy Englishmen who made the 'Grand Tour' of Europe at the time were thought by continentals to be eccentric, but this is surely an extreme example!

The day of the great open hearth with its ornamental fire-back was nearly at an end in English kitchens and enclosed grates gradually came into use. At first bars were fitted horizontally between the uprights

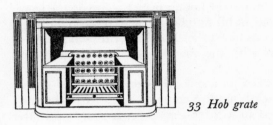

33 Hob grate

of the fire-dogs, to make a kind of basket called a 'dog-grate'. Later, in an attempt to reduce the lifting of heavy utensils, a 'hob-grate' developed which had, on each side, a flap or hob on which pans could be stood.

In 1775 there came to England from Bavaria a certain Count Rumford, who was very outspoken in his condemnation of the kitchen fireplaces in the houses where he stayed. He criticized the great loss of heat and the waste of fuel resulting from the fact that the fireplaces were not fully enclosed. Perhaps partly because of Rumford's criticisms, experiments were made with a hot-plate, a long, flat cast-iron plate set on a brick base. Under this hot-plate, at one end, was the fire-box and at the other end a vertical flue connected with a horizontal one, along which the hot gas from the fire could travel to the chimney and so heat the plate and the receptacles on it.

In 1780 a patent was taken out by a Mr Thomas Robinson for the first kitchen range, which had a cast-iron oven on one side and a boiler, for heating water, on the other. The oven was lined with bricks and mortar and had fillets along the sides for shelves to rest on. The early ranges made a great deal of smoke and used coal very extravagantly.

Whatever arrangements were made for cooking, Georgian kitchens must have been very dirty places, for great clouds of smoke covered everything with thick wood- and coal-dust. Mrs Hannah Glasse, in *The Art of Cookery Made Plain and Easy,* published in 1747, gave a dire warning about neglecting the cleaning of pots and pans. 'A whole family', she declared, 'died owing to verdigrease.' In fact, most cleaning was done by scouring the inside of the utensils with sand.

Roasting was done on a spit, as it had been for centuries. This was a long, pointed metal rod which rested on notches on the front of the kitchen fire-dogs and had a wheel fitted at one end. Some spits had additional spikes on each side to keep a joint steady, and poultry and tender meats were put in a basket- or cradle-spit.

Of course the wheel of a spit had to be kept continuously rotating, so as to ensure even cooking. The turning was often done by a 'turn-spit'—a small boy who turned the handle and made sure that the joint was 'done to a turn', as we still say. Dogs were also used for turning spits, and dog-power was later saved by the introduction of the 'chimney wheel' or 'smoke jack', which made the hot air from the fire do the work. The idea had been worked out in his notebooks by Leonardo da Vinci in the fifteenth century, but was new to an English writer who referred to 'a wooden jack that goes with the smoake, which indeed is very pretty'.

The fat from meat cooked on a spit dripped into a long, narrow iron trough standing underneath, and so came to be called 'dripping'. This was collected and stored in a three-legged 'greasepan' and later was used for making rushlights and candles.

The various types of spit were gradually superseded by spit-jacks. These consisted of a simple clockwork mechanism wound up by a key; it hung in front of the fire and had a hook underneath, from which the

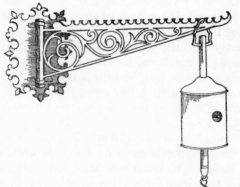

34 *Clockwork spit-jack*

joint was suspended on a chain. As the clockwork unwound, the chain and the joint both revolved in a horizontal plane, whereas the earlier spits had revolved vertically.

An improvement on the spit-jack was the Dutch oven, which was a dome-shaped metal cover, open towards the fire and extending nearly down to the floor, with an elaborate clockwork mechanism and hook inside it. The inside surface was kept bright and reflected the heat on to the meat. The dripping dripped through a hole in the bottom of the oven, into a pan underneath.

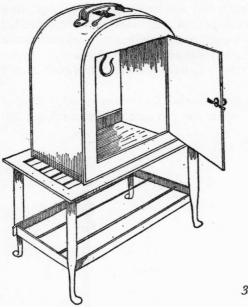

35 Dutch oven

In Hawkesworth's *Life* of Dr Swift, there is an amusing story of an encounter which the Dean had with his cook:

> The Dean had a kitchen wench for his cook, a woman of a large size, robust constitution and coarse features, her face very much seamed with the smallpox and furrowed by age; this woman he always distinguished by the name 'Sweetheart'.
> It happened one day that Sweetheart greatly over-roasted the only joint he had for dinner; upon which he sent for her, and with great coolness and gravity 'Sweetheart', he says, 'take this down to the kitchen and do it less.' She replied that was impossible. 'Pray, then,' said he, 'if you had roasted it too little, could you have done it more?' 'Yes' she said, easily could she have done that. 'Why, then, Sweetheart,' replied the Dean, 'let me advise you, if you must commit a fault, commit a fault that can be mended.'

36 Down-hearth toaster

A down-hearth toaster was a very efficient implement for toasting bread or slices of meat. It was made of iron, with a long handle swivelled to a stand, on each side of which were two semicircular hoops about an inch apart. The slice of bread or meat was put between the hoops and the toaster placed in front of the hearth; a twist of the swivel served to turn it without touching the food.

Another way of making toast was with a 'salamander', a kind of metal disc with a long handle, which was put into the fire until red-hot

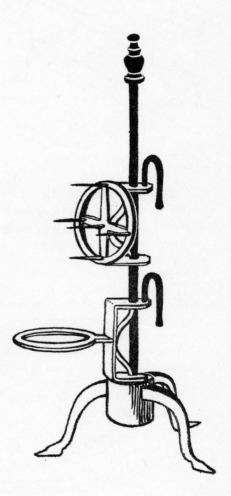

37 left *Hanging griller*
38 right *Griller with adaptable support for a basin or plate*

and then held close to a slice of bread. This was a new experience for a German visitor to England in 1782, who wrote:

> The slices of bread and butter, which they give you with your tea, are as thin as poppy leaves. But there is another kind of bread and butter usually eaten with tea, which is toasted by the fire and is incomparably good. You take one slice after the other and hold it to the heat till the butter is melted so that it penetrates a number of slices at once: this is called 'toast'.

Beer-warmers of iron or copper, either conical or slipper-shaped, were stood in the hearth to mull beer or ale. The slipper-shaped ones were more efficient as they stood on their soles, as it were, and did not have to be either propped up or held.

39 Beer warmers

Among many interesting inventories from the eighteenth century which are in the East Sussex Record Office, is one relating to a farmer who had possessed in his kitchen:

> Two Payer of Andirons Two Firepans one Payer of Tongs one Payer of Potthangers one Payer of Bellis Three Spitts Two Iron Candelsticks Two Iron Dripingpans one old Grigiron one Chopingknife one old Clevour one old Clock one old Warming pan one Payer of Stylliards one old Gunn Nyne Dishes of Pewter And A Pewter Tanker Two old Tables and Fine Old Joynd stools Fine old Chairs one Large Iron Skillet And one Small Brass Skillet one Old Iron kettle Three old Iron Porridgpotts one Old Settle And One old Buntinghutch and other Small Things.

Whoever made out the inventory after the farmer's death knew nothing of punctuation and his spelling, like that of everyone else at the time, was by inclination more than by rule.

All the pans, hobs, trivets, spits, toasters, salamanders and other implements used at the kitchen fireplace in Georgian times, and for centuries before that, seem to us to have been heavy and clumsy; but it is important to realize that in its time each new utensil was welcomed by housewives and cooks as a valuable labour-saving device. Women must often have been desperately tired, however, with lifting and carrying them.

The staple food, for much of the year, was still salted meat and fish. From the kitchen rafters there hung large hams in linen bags, and a wooden crate in which bread was safely kept away from the attentions of rats and mice. Large bunches of herbs hung there, too, sweetly scenting the air of the room.

Towns were growing so rapidly—even before the Industrial Revolution began—that the people could no longer, as before, live off the immediately adjacent countryside. London's meat *walked* to town from remote districts, so it was fresh on arrival but must have been tough after having been driven from Wales, from Cumberland, or Scotland. Poultry, too, came on foot, mostly from the flat counties of East Anglia. Fish could not walk, but often arrived stale and stinking; but later in the century canal transport helped in the provision of fresh food to all areas.

There was no control over the sale of milk. When it came from farm cows it was sometimes fresh, but often sour. Town cows were kept in such appallingly dirty conditions that their milk must have been the most dangerous of foods. Milkmaids carrying open cans of milk on their heads went from door to door; the open cans protected their heads from the slops and rubbish thrown from upstairs windows, but no housewife or cook can have bought milk with any confidence.

Country housewives often sent to London for supplies not easily available locally. There were carriers who travelled between London and provincial towns, as we can see from this letter sent by Mrs Purefoy on February 6th 1747:

Mr Willson,

        I desire you will send mee

        One pound of the best Bohea Tea

        Half a pound of the best green Tea

        Two pounds of the best Coffeeberries

        A quarter of a pound of nutmegs

        Two ounces of mace

        A quarter of an hundred of the best treble refined Loaf

                               sugar

        A quarter of an hundred of Household sugar about

                       6 pence a pound

Half a quarter of an hundred of Polish starch
Half a quarter of an hundred of Rice
Send these by ye Buckingham carrier . . . send your
Bill with them and will order you payment. The last Bohea Tea
was so ordinary I could not drink it, my neighbours had as
good for six shillings a pound. The last hundredweight of
Raisins you send were so bad they spoiled the Liquor they were
made on. I hope you will send no more bad Goods, I have had
no reason to complain till now, tho' I have dealt at yr shop these
forty years and am

Your humble serft

E.P.

P.S. If you can't conveniently send them on Tuesday Mr Jones
ye carrier sets out of London on Saturday mornings early.

Sir Frederick Eden, in his report on 'The State of the Poor'
stated that cheese, bread and tea were the staple diet of the poor in mid-
Georgian times, just as beef, bread and beer had been in the sixteenth
century. Cheese was also enjoyed as an addition to the large meals of the
wealthy, so many of whom were now city-dwellers. As a result of this
fact cheese, which had previously been a local product with only a local
reputation, began to be sold in the towns by the name of its place of
origin. By the end of the century there is mention of Cheshire, Cheddar,
Wiltshire, Double Gloucester, Somerset and Stilton cheese. Cheese-
making, which had always been the domestic responsibility of the
farmer's wife, now began to be a profitable sideline to farming.

Potatoes were a fairly common vegetable in England by this
time, but in Scotland there was great reluctance to growing them as a
field crop. They had been cultivated in a few private gardens in the
beginning of the century, and used as delicacies, but the common
people regarded them with suspicion, under the belief that farmers were
going to deprive them of their proper nourishment—oats. A Scots
writer on husbandry instructed that—'The commonest way they are
made use of are boyled and broken, and stewed with butter and new
milk. Yea, some make bread with them by mixing them with oats or
barley meal . . . others parboyle them and bake them with apples after
the manner of tarts'.

However, successive years of bad corn harvest helped to overcome prejudice and by 1750 potatoes were in common use in Scotland.

Kitchen staff in a great household shared the responsibility of
collecting ice in winter, to replenish the ice-houses in which food was
kept cold in summer. Sheets of ice were collected from ponds and lakes,
packed in salt and wrapped in strips of flannel, or between layers of
stone, and stored in underground vaults. Winters were much more

severe than they are now and there were not many years when ice-houses could not be filled.

There was a great deal of gluttony and overeating among those Englishmen who could afford it. Immense improvements in agriculture towards the end of the century gradually made it possible for all but the poorest to have fresh meat all the year round, and our growing overseas trade was reflected in the plentiful supply of sugar, spices and citrus fruits. Hothouse fruit was very expensive, but outdoor fruit growing was increasing. Mrs Purefoy had, in her garden in Bucking-hamshire, nectarines, golden pippin apples, several varieties of pears, black-heart cherries and black grapes. Baskets of fruit were frequently given as presents and in the country 'strawberry parties' were often held.

French cooking had been the pattern for the western world in the seventeenth century, but Georgian cooks developed an anti-French outlook and felt confident of the value of plainer, English ways of pre-paring food. Mrs Hannah Glasse was one of many writers of cook-books who disapproved of French cooking. 'So much is the blind folly of this age', she wrote, 'that some would rather be imposed upon by a French booby than give encouragement to a good English cook.'

The under-servants in a large house were sometimes overworked and even beaten, but they seldom lacked for good food. In 1772 the Duke of Bedford had an indoor staff of forty-two at Woburn; they were evidently well treated, for many of them remained in his service for a great many years. In farmhouses servants ate in the kitchen with their employers, having the same plentiful fare, but a maid alone in a small house often had a very unhappy time. A writer commented towards the end of the century: 'I have seen the slavery of the West Indies and the slavery of the galleys, but the veriest slaves I have seen are the all-work servants of London.'

In a large household the servants were now usually supervised by a 'house-keeper', though the Duke of Bedford still kept a house-steward. This letter, sent by a gentleman to his steward in 1705, shows how varied were the responsibilities of that office:

> I shall now soone be with you in Bedfordshire, if God permitt
> and therefore doe admonish you to gett the house in order for
> my Reception, that is ayred and cleane. I shall bring downe
> with me two freinds besides my son Jack soe that accommodation
> must be found and the Beds extream drye and wholesome. I
> expect to find the gardens in good Condition in every particular
> and the fontaines perfected. . . . Remember about getting inn
> a sufficient stock of Oates and Beanes for the service of the
> stables as you did the last yeare and lett me find you loose

noe time in this soe necessary a worke. I thinke you send upp but very few sparagrasse. Lett me know your proceedings in all manner of businesse. Your freind John Ashburnham.

A housekeeper had the charge and supervision of all the women servants, and in many households she was responsible for appointing and dismissing them and paying their wages. She saw to it that they did their various jobs and kept the house well and, in addition to her more obvious duties, she had to be something of a doctor. In *The Compleat Gentlewoman*, published in 1711, Hannah Woolley states that housekeepers must have 'a competent knowledge of physick and chyrurgery, that they may be able to help their maimed, sick and indigent neighbours, for commonly all good and charitable ladies make this a part of their Housekeepers business.'

Early in the century an advertisement in a weekly pamphlet offered a paragon as a housekeeper:

If any wants a Housekeeper I can help to a Gentlewoman who through misfortune of a bad husband is reduced. She is sober, diligent and careful, and has been used to all manner of business for a Housekeeper, as also to rise early and sit up late.

There were continual complaints about servants. Daniel Defoe had this to say about them:

The most pernicious are those who beggar you by inches. If a maid is a downright thief she strips you at once and you know your loss; but these retail pilferers waste you insensibly and you hardly miss it; your substance shall decay to such a degree that you must have a very good bottom indeed not to feel the ill effects of such mouths in your family. Tea, sugar and wine or any such trifling commodities are reckoned no the less, if they do not directly take your pewter from your shelves or your linen from your drawers.

But even in a kind home maids were expected to work very hard indeed, as we can see from another letter written by Mrs Purefoy in 1744:

Mrs Ffenimore,
I had notice that your Daughter desired to come and live with mee. She must milk 3 or 4 cows and understand how to manage the Dairy and know how to boyll and roast ffowls and butcher's meatt. Wee wash once a month, she and the washerwoman wash all but the small linnen, and next day she and the washerwoman wash the Buck [the heavier clothes]. She helps the other maid wash the rooms when they are done,

she makes the Garrett beds and cleans them, and cleans the great stairs and scours all the irons and scours the Pewter in use, and we have a woman to help when 't is all done. There is a very good time to do all this provided she is a good servant, and when she has done her worke she sits down to spin. . . .

No mention of time off!

In some households servants had to obey very strict rules. In the servants' hall at Clandon Park, in Surrey, is the original eighteenth-century notice which states:

RULES to be Observed in this HALL

d.

1. WHOEVER is last at Breakfast to clear the Table and put the Copper, Horns, Salt, Pepper etc, in their proper places, or forfeit } 3

2. THE servants hall Cloth laid for Dinner by 1 o'Clock, and not omit laying the Salt, Pepper, and Spoons } 3

3. THE housekeepers room Knives to be clean'd ev'ry day by the Usher of this hall } 3

4. THAT if any Person be heard to Swear, or Use any Indecent language at any time when the Cloth is on the table, He is to forfeit } 3

5. WHOEVER leaves any thing belonging to their Dress or any Wearing Apparel out of their proper places } 3

6. THAT no one be suffered to Play at Cards in the Hall, before six o'Clock in the Evening } 3

7. WHOEVER leaves any Pieces of Bread at Breakfast, Dinner, or Supper } 1

8. THAT if any one shall be observed cleaning livery clothes, or leather breeches, at any time of Meals; or shall leave any dirt after cleaning them at any time } 3

9. THAT the Usher to have the Hall decently Swept, and the dirt taken away before dinner time } 3

10. THAT no one shall put any kind of provisions in any Cupboard or Drawer in the Hall after their meals, but shall return it from whence they had it } 3

11. THAT the Table Cloth shall after all meals be folded up, and put in the drawer for that purpose } 3

12. THAT if any one be observed wipeing their knives in the table cloth at any time } 3

13. THAT if any stable or other servant take any plates to the stable, or be seen to set them for the Dogs to eat off } 3

14. THAT no wearing apparel to hang in the Hall, but shall be put in the Closets for that Purpose ⎫ 3

15. ALL stable and other servants to come to dinner with their Coats on ⎫ 3

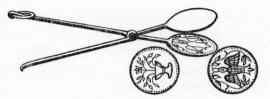

40 Wafering iron, for making waffles

Until the late eighteenth century domestic labour had for centuries been recruited by recommendation, or hired at 'mop fairs', where the prospective servants presented themselves with emblems of their trade—carters with whips, maids with mops, gardeners with spades, and so on. But in a city this would not do and in 1764 a Mrs Raffald put up a notice in her confectioner's shop in Manchester:

Mrs Raffald begs to inform . . . her friends . . . that she supplies Families with Servants, for any place, at ONE shilling each. Masters and Servants, therefore, at any Distance, may be supplied on the shortest notice, by directing (Post paid) to Mrs Raffald at the REGISTER OFFICE in Fennel Street, Manchester. No servant need apply without they can have a character from the Person they have served.

In the *Housekeeping Book of Susanna Whatman,* wife of a wealthy paper manufacturer in the middle of the century, we read instructions for her housekeeper and other servants:

The first thing a housekeeper should teach a new servant is to carry her candle upright. . . . One of the most useful common directions next to carrying a candle upright is that of putting away chairs, tables and anything that goes next to a wall, with a hand behind it. For want of this trifling attention, great pieces are frequently knocked out of the stucco, and the backs of chairs, if bending, leave a mark on the wall.

Mrs Whatman was evidently a strict, as well as a careful housewife. Among the instructions to housemaids, she wrote:

The books in the library are not to be meddled with, but they may be dusted as far as a wing of a goose will go.

To whisk all the window curtains every Saturday.

To use a painter's brush to all the ledges, window frames and furniture.

Never to use a hard brush to any mahogany carving that has been neglected and the dust suffered to settle.

To rise on Tuesday mornings to wash her own things and the dusters, and help wash stockings. . . . To mend the towels and her Master's common stockings of an evening.

Venetian blinds. When let down, to pull the longest string to turn or close them quite. Otherwise the sun will come through the laths.

In another book of *Domestic Management,* written at the end of the century, the author cautioned his readers about the carelessness of some housemaids towards the furniture:

I have seen a strong country wench, from a conception that hard rubbing is necessary, raise a cabriole chair on one leg and, in order to rub the opposite leg, lean on it with that force as to make the whole frame crack, and rub a slight table till it has given way under her heavy hand.

And there were sometimes more serious complaints about servants, as we see from this letter written in 1710:

The Keeper is such a dreadful fellow that for my part I can't immagin what the maids will doe with him, for he went to the Beer Seller and he is more drunk than yesterday, for above three hours with small Beare, as there won't be a drop left when I goe away; and because the Cooke lock'd the Seller Doore in the afternoon, as I order'd her, Roberts being gon out, he nail'd up all the Larders and the Cook's Chamber doore, and indeed you never saw so strange a fellow in your life, and the gardener is as bad. . . .

A vituperative correspondence between two titled eighteenth-century ladies concerning a servant, sounds amusing to our ears. Lady Seymour was the grandmother of Sheridan, the playwright:

1. Lady Seymour presents her compliments to Lady Shuckburgh, and would be obliged to her for the character of Mary Steadman, who states that she has lived twelve months, and still is, in Lady Shuckburgh's establishment. Can Mary Steadman cook plain dishes well, and make bread, and is she honest, sober, willing, cleanly and good tempered: Lady Seymour will also like to know the reasons she leaves Lady

Shuckburgh's house. Direct under care to Lord Seymour, Meriden Bradley, Wiltshire.

2. Lady Shuckburgh presents her compliments to Lady Seymour; her ladyship's letter dated October 28th only reached her yesterday, November 3rd. Lady Shuckburgh was unacquainted with the name of the kitchen maid until mentioned by Lady Seymour, as it is her custome neither to apply for, nor give, characters to any of the under-servants, this being always done by the housekeeper, Mrs Couch, and this was well known to the young woman. Therefore Lady Shuckburgh is surprised at her referring any lady to her for a character. Lady Shuckburgh, keeping a professed cook, as well as a housekeeper in her establishment, it is not very probable she herself should know anything of the abilities or merits of the under-servants; she is therefore unable to reply to Lady Seymour's note. Lady Shuckburgh cannot imagine Mary Steadman to be capable of cooking anything, except for the servants' hall table.

3. November 4th Lady Seymour presents her compliments to Lady Shuckburgh and begs she will order her housekeeper, Mrs Couch, to send the girl's character, otherwise another young woman will be sought for elsewhere, as Lady Seymour's children cannot remain without their dinners because Lady Shuckburgh, keeping a professed cook and housekeeper, thinks a knowledge of the details of her establishment beneath her notice. Lady Seymour understands from Steadman that, in addition to her other talents, she was actually capable of cooking food for the little Shuckburghs to partake of when hungry.

4. Madam—Lady Shuckburgh has directed me to acquaint you that she declines answering your note, the vulgarity of which she thinks beneath her contempt, and although it may be a characteristic of the Sheridans to be vulgar, coarse and witty, it is not that of a lady, unless she chances to have been 'born in a garret and bred in a kitchen'. Mary Steadman informs me that your ladyship does not keep either a cook or housekeeper, and that you only require a girl who can cook a mutton chop, if so, I apprehend that Mary Steadman, or any other scullion, will be found fully equal to the establishment of the Queen of Beauty. I am, madam, your Ladyship's etc. etc. Elizabeth Couch.

One servant in a London household was of a literary inclination and described his duties thus:

As soon as laziness will let me,
I rise from bed and down I set me

To cleaning glasses, knives and plates,
And such-like dirty work as that
Which (by the bye) is what I hate.
Here some short time doth interpose
Till warm effluvias greet my nose
Which from the spits and kettles fly
Declaring dinner-time is nigh;
To lay the cloth I now prepare
With uniformity and care;
In order knives and forks are laid,
With folded napkins, salt and bread.
The side-boards glittering too, appear
With plate and glass and china-ware.
Then ale and beer and wine decanted,
And all things ready which are wanted
The smoking dishes enter in
To stomachs sharp a grateful scene.
Which on the table being placed,
And some few ceremonies past,
They all sit down and fall to eating,
While I behind stand silent waiting.

Dean Swift's cynical *Directions to Servants* emphasizes the habitual dishonesty, cunning and carelessness of eighteenth-century servants; here he gives us a depressing picture of the kitchen of a Georgian house:

Let it be a constant rule that no chair, stool or table in the
servants' hall or kitchen shall have above three legs, which
has been the ancient and constant practice in all the families
I ever knew and is said to be founded upon two reasons: first
to show that servants are ever in a tottering condition; secondly
it was thought a point of humility that the servants' chairs and
tables should have at least one leg fewer than those of their
masters.

A constant source of argument in the kitchen quarters was the coming and going of charwomen. Maids were warned to beware of gossip recounted by these doubtful characters, and also of the woman who went round from house to house calling 'Kitchen stuff ha' ye, maids?' which can be seen in woodcuts illustrating the cries of London. Servants must often have been tempted to sell or barter 'kitchen stuff' to which they had no legal right.

One of the kitchen 'perks' which was quite legitimate, was the sale of used tea-leaves, which the poor bought for a penny or two at the back doors of well-to-do houses. Tea was heavily taxed and very expensive; the small 'caddy'[1] was kept under lock and key by the housewife or her housekeeper and its contents rationed as required. So much tea was drunk in England that some families were said to have ruined themselves with it.

Another visitor to the kitchen door was the woman who sold sand, used for cleaning and polishing metal, as we hear in an old folksong:

Who liveth so merry in all this land
As doth the poor widow who selleth the sand?
And ever she singeth as I can guess,
'Will ye buy any sand, any sand, mistress?'

We learn about rush-making from a letter written on November 1st 1775, by Gilbert White to a friend; this letter is about...

the use of rushes instead of candles, which I am well aware prevails in many districts besides this. . . . The proper species of rush for this purpose seems to be the Juncus conglomeratus, or common soft rush. These rushes are in best condition in the height of summer . . . the largest and longest are best. Decayed labourers, women and children make it their business to procure and prepare them. As soon as they are cut, they must be flung into water and kept there, for otherwise they will dry and shrink and the peel will not run. At first a person would find it no easy matter to divest a rush of its peel or rind, so as to leave one regular, narrow, even rib from top to bottom that may support the pith. . . .

When these Junci are prepared, they must lie out on the grass to be bleached, and take the dew for some nights, and afterwards be dried in the sun.

When dried, the rushes had to be dipped into scalding fat and White reports that...

the careful wife of an industrious Hampshire labourer obtains all her fat for nothing, for she saves the scummings of her bacon-pot for this use. . . . Where hogs are not much in use, and especially by the sea-side, the coarser animal-oils will come very cheap. A pound of common grease may be procured for fourpence and about six pounds of grease will dip a pound of

---

[1] The word 'caddy' is derived from *kati*, an Eastern measure of weight. At first they were called 'tea-chests' and usually matched the furniture in the dining room.

rushes, and one pound of rushes may be bought for one shilling. . . . If men that keep bees will mix a little wax with the grease . . . it will render it more clearly and make the rushes burn longer.

A good rush, which measured in length two feet four inches and a half, burnt only three minutes short of an hour . . .

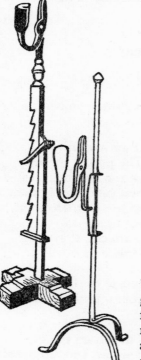

in a pound of dry rushes, avoirdupois . . . we found upwards of one thousand six hundred individuals. . . . An experienced old housekeeper assures me that one pound and a half of rushes completely supplies his family the year round, since working people burn no candles in the long days, because they rise and go to bed by daylight. . . . Little farmers use rushes much in the short days both morning and evening, in the dairy and kitchen; but the very poor, who are always the worst economists, and therefore must continue very poor, buy a halfpenny candle every evening, which in their blowing, open rooms does not burn much more than two hours.

*41 Standing rushlight-
and candle-holders*

The rush still had to be lit from a tinder-box which contained a piece of flint, a hand-grip of iron, some pieces of charred rag and a flat metal plate to extinguish the smouldering material. Housewives saved old linen to be used as tinder and this had to be shredded and dried in the kitchen ready to use. Small tongs called 'brand tongs' were often kept by the kitchen fire, as a means of obtaining a light without the bother of lighting tinder.

Getting a light could be a very difficult matter, as Dr Johnson's Boswell described in 1763:

I determined to sit up all night, which I accordingly did and wrote a great deal. About two o'clock in the morning I inadvertently snuffed out my candle, and as my fire was long before black and cold, I was in a great dilemma how to proceed. Downstairs did I softly and silently step to the kitchen. But, alas, there was as little fire there as upon the icy mountains of Greenland. With a tinder box is a light struck every morning to kindle the fire, which is put out at night. But this tinder box I could not see, nor knew where to find. I was now filled with gloomy ideas of the terrors of the night. . . . I went up to my room, sat quietly until I heard the watchman calling 'past three o'clock'. I then called to him to knock at the door of the house where I lodged. He did so, and I opened to him and got my candle re-lumed without danger. Thus was I relieved and continued busy until eight the next day.

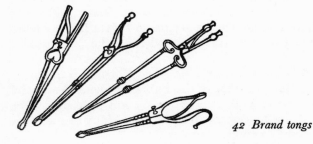

42 Brand tongs

Eighteenth-century housekeepers carefully kept their favourite recipes, for both cooking and cleaning, in note-books which were handed down from mother to daughter. E. Smith, in the Preface to *The Compleat Houseweife or Accomplish'd Gentlewoman's Companion,* of 1744, has this to say about French styles:

> What you will find in the following Sheets, are Directions for dressing after the best, most natural and wholesome Manner, such Provisions as are the Products of our own Country; and in such manner as is most agreeable to English Palates; saving, that I have so far temporized, as since we have, to our Disgrace, so fondly admired the French Tongue, French Modes, and also French Messes, to present you now and then with such Receipts of the French Cookery as I think may not be disagreeable to English Palates.

We see how versatile a housewife had to be, from the title page of Sarah Harrison's *Housekeeper's Pocket Book.* As well as giving us 'About twelve hundred curious and uncommon receipts', she gives 'Directions for Making all sorts of Wine, Mead, Cyder etc. and distilling strong waters, for brewing ale, Small Beer and for Managing and Breeding Poultry to Advantage', and then adds 'Several useful Family Receipts for taking out Stains, preserving Furniture, cleaning Plate, taking Iron Moulds out of Linen. As also easy Tables of Sums ready cast up, from one Farthing to one Pound, for the Use of Those not conversant in Arithmetic.'

Mrs Harrison also gives advice about 'Every one their own Physician; or Charity made pleasant by Relieving their own Family or poor neighbouring People, by Cheap, easy and safe Remedies'. And, in support of the importance of the housewifely arts she declared firmly: 'Certainly no Art whatsoever, relating to terrestrial Things, ought to claim in Preference to that which makes Life easy.'

There was a great deal of borrowing among compilers of cook-books of the period, and there is a mystery surrounding the authorship of *The Art of Cooking Made Plain and Easy ... by a Lady*. In 1760 there appeared *The Servant's Directory* by H. Glasse, author of *The Art of Cookery*. There is more than a suspicion that a literary hoax was involved and bibliographers still argue whether the famous Mrs Glasse ever existed.

A different kind of book entitled *The School of Arts* and intended 'for the use, emolument and pleasure of the Public in General and the encouragement of arts, manufacture and science', was published after the foundation of the Royal Society of Arts in 1754. Many of the ideas given would be of interest to a careful housewife:

Chinese method of mending china
Boil a piece of flint glass in river water, to clean it five or six minutes, beat it to fine powder, and grind it well with the white of an egg, and it joins China without rivetting, so that no art can break it again in the same place. You are to observe, the composition is to be ground extremely fine on a painter's stone.

To take spots or stains out of linen
Take the juice of lemon and red onion mixed together, put to it a little salt and heat it gently over a fire, and then dip the part that is stained often in it: let it then dry, and get in readiness a hot lather of soap and water, to wash it immediately; and doing so in two or three washings it will quite disappear.

To discover whether flour be adulterated with whitening or chalk
Mix with the flour some juice of lemon or good vinegar; if the flour is pure, they will remain together at rest, but if there be a mixture of whitening or chalk, a fermentation or working like yeast will ensue. The adulterated meal is whiter and heavier than the good. The quantity that an ordinary tea-cup will contain, has been found to weigh more than the quantity of genuine flour by four drachms and nineteen grains troy.

To make a continual light by night
Take one ounce of the oil of almonds, put half a drachm of phosphorus and two or three grains of the flour of sulphur into

94

it; hold it in a gentle warmth to dissolve, then shake the
bottle and draw your cork, and you will have a fine glow-worm
light. If you rub a little on the nost, or any other part it will
appear all in a flame.

To clean boot tops
Boil one quart of milk, let it stand till cold; to which put one
ounce of oil of vitriol, one ounce of spirits of salts, and shake
them well together; then add one ounce of red lavender. You
may put half a pint of vinegar, with the white of an egg
beat to a froth.

Remedies against fleas
Fumigation with brimstone, or the fresh leaves of penny-royal
sewed in a bag, and laid on a bed, will have the desired
effect.

It is fortunate for us that a certain lady of title who lived in
Brighthelmstone—as Brighton was then called—employed as butler
one Thomas Newington. We know nothing about the lady herself
except that in 1719 her butler wrote out for his mistress a collection
of recipes 'which were the Palladium of Many Noble Familyes'. These
are culinary, cosmetic and medicinal recipes, written in a charming
style, without punctuation and with very varied spelling; many have
a remarkable simplicity and optimism, others are complicated, others
brutal:

For Chopt Lips
Take your own Watter and boyle it to a surrup with sum
Duble Refine lofe Sugar and so keep it for your use.

To take away Freckles in the Face
Take one Pint of White Wine Vinegar and put it into a glass
with six Oaken Apples and a few elder leaves. Set it in the sun
and wash your Face therewith.

For ye Naile growing into one Toe
Take strong wine Vinegar and Dip lint into it and put it upon
the place and it will soften the Naile that you may cut it out.

To Kill and Roast a Pigg
Take your Pigg and hold the head down a Payle of cold Watter
untill strangeled then hang him up buy the heals and fley him
then open him then chine him down the back as you doe a
porker first cuting of his head then cut him in fower quarters
then lard two of the quarters with lemon peele and the other
two with tope of Time then spit and roast them. The head

requears more roasting than the braines with a little Saige and grave for sauce.

To Pickle Nerstusan Seeds and Flowers

Gather the buds whilst they are greene with the Stalkes an Inch long Take a quart of Clarret and a quart of white wine Vinegar and som cloves and mace, if you please a prity deale of salt and make it boyle and then take it of and let it stand till it be cold. And put the flowers and the buds into an Earthen pott and power the pickle upon them and stop it with a cork and cover it with a lether and keep them for your use.

What fun it must have been! what variety, excitement and interest for servants and children! what therapy in concocting a complicated 'Receipt for the Surrup of Long Life to be done in the Moone of May'!

Modern psychology finds that a busy, active, interested person is less likely to fall ill. Thomas Newington knew something about this, too, for one would surely not have *time* to be ill if one were to prepare 'a Snayle Watter good in a Consumption or Jaundis to clear the Skin or Revive ye Spirrits':

Take a Peck of Garden Snayles in their Shells. Gather them as near as you can out of lavender or Rosemary and not in trees or grass. Wash them in a Tubb three times in Beere, then make your Chimney very clean and power out a bushall of charcole and when they are well kindled make a great hole with a fire shovell and put in your Snayles and Put in some of your cleane burnt coals among them and let roast till they leave makeing a noise, then you must take them forth with a knife and cleane them with a cleane Cloathpick and wipe away the coales and green froth that will be upon them. Then beat them in a mortar shells and all. Take also a Quart of Earth-worms, slitt and scower them with salt, then wash them in whitewine till you have taken away all the filth from them, and put them into a stone Mortar and beat them to pieces. Then take a sweet, clean Iron pott which you will sett your limbeck on, then 2 Ms of Angellica and lay it in the bottom of your Pott and 2 Ms of Sallendine, on the top of that putt in 2 quarts of Rosemary Flowers, Bearsfoot, Egrimony, the redest Dock/Roots you can get, the barbery bark, Wood Sorrell, bettony, of each three handfulls, 1 handfull of Rue, of Flengreek and Tumerick of each one ounce well beaten. Then lay your Snayles and wormes on the top of your herbs and flowers and

96

power upon them the strongest Ale you can gett fower gallons, and two gallons of the best sack and let it stand all night or longer stirring Divers times. In the morning put in two ounces of Cloves twelve ounces of hartshorne, six ounces of ivory, the waight of two shillings in Saffron. The Cloves must be bruised. You must not stir it after these last things are in. Then set it on your limbeck and close it fast with Rye Past and receive your water in Pintes. The first is strongest and so smaller, the smallest may be mended by putting in some of the strongest. When you use it take three spoonfulls of beere or Ale to two spoonfulls of the strongest and to this three quarts of cowslips flowers one quart of Buglose and buridg flowers and 3 Ms of liverworth. And if you will you may putt in 3 Gallons of Sack and two of Ale only, and draw it no longer than it will burn, and put into every quart glass 3d in safforon and three ounces of cloves. If you will you should feed your Snayles with sallendine and barberry leaves and bough, and then wash them in new milk fower times and then in a Tubb of strong Ale so that they may be very cleane and then burn them.

The water supply in many towns was still very poor. In York the quality was so poor that most houses had large pots standing in the kitchen quarters, in which water was left to settle for a day or two before use. In 1765 Manchester issued a proclamation forbidding the drowning of cats and dogs, or the washing of dirty linen, in the reservoir that supplied the town! It is not surprising that people brewed their own beer and that even children drank what was known as 'small beer'.

At the beginning of the century, tea was a rarity and a precious luxury of which friends would send a pound from abroad as a costly gift. In time, however, it became less expensive, and by the end of the century it had become the national drink.

In 1729 an eminent Scot was lamenting the sadly changed times:

When I came to my friend's house of a morning, I used to be asked if I had my morning draught yet? I am now asked if I have had my tea? And in lieu of . . . a dram of good wholesome Scots spirits, there is now the tea-kettle put to the fire, the tea-table and silver and china equipage brought in, and marmalade and cream.

When gradually beer gave way to tea, people transferred the terms for brewing their home-made ale to the process of making their tea; 'mashing' meant adding hot water to the malt, and came to mean infusing tea, and 'brewing tea' is an expression still sometimes used.

That there were many different qualities of tea drunk, is evident

from this description written by the rector of a village in Berkshire in
1787:

> Beer has been these many years far beyond their [his parishioners']
> ability to use in common. Tea with bread furnishes one meal
> for a whole family every day, at no greater expense than about
> one shilling a week at an average. . . . You exclaim Tea is a
> luxury. If you mean fine hyson tea, sweetened with refined
> sugar and softened with cream, I readily admit it to be so.
> But *this* is not the tea of the poor. Spring water, just coloured
> with a few leaves of the lowest price tea, and sweetened with
> the brownest sugar, is the luxury of which you reproach them.

Smuggling was very general in Britain at this time. It added
interest to people's lives, reduced the cost of domestic necessities, and
was regarded by everyone as entirely innocent. Parson Woodforde, who
was, by definition, a man of some reputation, noted in his diary on
March 29th 1777:

> Andrews the smuggler brought me this night about 11 o'clock
> a bagg of Hyson Tea 6 pound weight. He frightened us a little
> by whistling under the parlour window just as we were going
> to bed. I gave him Geneva [gin] and paid him for the tea at
> 10/6d per pound.

Conditions were particularly bad for poor country families during
the last quarter of the century, and especially in the south. In the north
food supplies were more secure: the labourer could still keep a cow and
gather turf on land still unenclosed; he did not rely on wheat for his
bread, but preferred oatmeal. In the south the poor could not graze
animals on open land, but had to pay for pasture and in consequence
many labourers could not keep a cow. Fuel was so scarce and dear that
families often shared a cooking fire, and the potato was used mainly by
well-to-do households and not by the poor as a cheaper substitute for
wheat, as occurred in the next century. In 1796 the Government allowed
the import of duty-free rice and maize from Carolina, but the labourer's
wife did not know how to cook either, and nobody told her.

Eighteenth-century Virginian diarists often recorded details
about farming operations in the colony, but no housewife's diary seems
to have survived. Yet it was she, after all, who was responsible for the
house, the 'dependencies' (as bake-house, dairy, brew-house, smoke-
house and slaves' quarters were called) and of the kitchen, the kitchen-
garden and poultry yard.

The plantations of Virginia's gentlemen were worlds of their
own, directed with the same taste and ability and detailed interest as
those of English gentlemen. Apart from salt, spices, molasses, tea and

coffee, the land provided everything. Timber, iron-ore and brick-making clays were the raw materials for innumerable domestic installations carried out by carpenters, masons, wheelwrights, coopers and blacksmiths. Many a large plantation had its shoemaker, its spinners and weavers, seedsmen, gardeners, brewers, bakers and cooks 'within themselves'.

The first known cook-book published in British America was E. Smith's *Compleat Housewife*, which appeared in Williamsburg in 1742. The question of how written directions could be followed in kitchens where illiterate servants did the cooking, was answered by an old slave who recalled that, during his childhood, his mother was pastry-cook to Mr and Mrs Thomas Jefferson at Monticello. He remembered that 'Mrs Jefferson would come out there with a cookbook in her hand and read out of it to my mother, how to make cakes, tarts and so on'.

A North American writer described his home in New England at the end of the eighteenth century:

The kitchen was large, fully twenty feet square, with a fireplace six feet wide and four feet deep. On one side it looked out upon the garden, the squashes and cucumbers climbing up and forming festoons over the door. The kitchen was in fact the most comfortable room in the house, cool in summer and perfumed with the breath of the garden and orchard; in the winter, with its roaring blaze of hickory, it was a cosy resort, defying the bitterest blasts of the season. . . . The cellar, extending under the whole house . . . was by no means the least important part of the house. In the autumn [it contained] barrels of beef and pork, barrels of cider, bins of potatoes, turnips, beets, carrots and cabbages. The garret, which was of huge dimensions, at the same time displayed a labyrinth of dried pumpkins, peaches, and apples, hung in festoons upon the rafters, amid bunches of summer savory, boneset, fennel and other herbs—the floor being occupied by heaps of wool, flax, tow and the like. . . .
Our bread was of rye, tinged with Indian meal. Wheat bread was reserved for the sacrament and company; proof not of its superiority but of its scarcity and subsequent estimation. All the vegetables came from our garden and farm. The fuel was supplied by our own woods—sweet-scented hickory, snapping chestnut, odoriferous oak, and reeking, fizzling ash—the hot juice of the latter being a sovereign antidote for the ear ache. These were laid in huge piles, all alive with sap, on the tall, gaunt andirons. . . . The building of the fire was a real architectural achievement, favoured by the wide yawning

fireplace, and was always begun by day-break. There was first a back-log, from fifteen to four and twenty inches in diameter and five feet long, imbedded in the ashes; then came a top-log, then a fore-stick, then a middle-stick, and then a heap of kindlings, reaching from the bowels down to the bottom. A-top of all was a pyramid of smaller fragments, artfully adjusted, with spaces for the blaze. . . . Friction matches had not then been sent from the regions of brimstone, to enable every boy or beggar to carry a conflagration in his pockets. If there were no coals left from last night's fire and none to be borrowed from the neighbours, resort was had to flint, steel, and tinder-box. Often when the fire was dull, and the steel soft, and the tinder damp, the striking of fire was a task requiring both energy and patience.

Making beds was a complicated business, as a writer explains when describing his life as a child in Vermont at the turn of the century:

Everybody slept on cornhusk ticks with feather beds on top; I never seed a mattress until I was quite a young man. The ticks rested on corn beds. Instead of a bedspring with slats underneath, they had cord strung between the bed rails. It practically took a mechanic to put a cord bed together; the ropes was laced back and forth crisscross, and after a while they would stretch out and sag down. Then you took a bed key, a two-inch square block about a foot and a half long, with a slot cut into one end to catch the rope, and a wooden crossbar at the other end to give you leverage; you give a twist and pulled up the slack in the ropes one at a time until they was taut again.

Until the end of the eighteenth century, lightness in the very popular baked pies, tarts and breads could only be achieved by laboriously beating eggs into dough or by adding yeast. In the seventeen-nineties pearl-ash was discovered in America and large quantities exported to Europe. It was not until the eighteen-fifties that baking powder was commercially produced in Boston, and this transformed baking methods.

There is an interesting description of a Thanksgiving dinner in New England during the Revolution in a letter written in 1779:

All the baking of pies and cakes was done at our house and we had the big oven heated and filled twice each day for 3 days before it was all done. Everything was good though we did have to do without some things that ought to be used . . . of course we had no Roast Beef. None of us have tasted Beef these three years back as it all must go to the Army and too little they get, poor fellows . . . a vegetable which I do not believe you have yet seen. Uncle Simeon had imported the Seeds from England just before the war began and only this year was there enough for Table use. It is called Sellery and you eat it without cooking.

George and Martha Washington always tried to spend the Christmas season together. Dinner at Mount Vernon was customarily served at three o'clock in the afternoon—an hour about which the General was altogether precise. He was likely to tell late guests: 'Gentlemen . . . I have a cook who never asks whether the company has come, but whether the hour has come.' Martha was equally punctual. In 1790 she concluded an evening party promptly at nine o'clock by rising and saying to her company, 'The General always retires at nine, and I usually precede him.'

A note in a colonial housewife's diary of November 23rd 1770 expressed frustrations often experienced by housewives of all countries at some time or another:

I never knew the like of my family for finding fault. At the same time they will not mend things when they might if they could. Everyone speaks well of my table, but they who constantly live at it. If the meat is very fine, it is not done, says one, altho Perhaps nobody eat hartier of it. . . . If the Sallat is fine, the melted butter it is mixed up with is rank altho every mouthfull of sallat is devoured . . . and so the good folk go on disparaging and devouring.

9

The Nineteenth Century

THE nineteenth century was a time of great prosperity among the upper and middle classes in England. Servants were still plentiful and even a comparatively simple household would have at least one maid. The principal rooms in a grand house were large and spacious, but the attics and basements, where the servants lived, were dark and damp. A continental visitor wrote describing the kitchen quarters of a wealthy house at which he had stayed in early Victorian days:

The servants live in a large room in a remote part of the house, generally on the ground floor where all, male and female, eat together, and where the bells of the whole house are placed. They are suspended in a row on the wall numbered so that it is immediately seen in what room anyone has rung; a sort of pendulum is attached to each, which continues to vibrate for about ten minutes after the sound has ceased to remind the sluggish of their duty. The females of the establishment have also a large common room, in which, when they have nothing else to do, they sew, knit or spin. Close to this is a closet for washing the glass and china, which comes within their province. . . . Immediately adjoining that of the housekeeper is a room where coffee is made and the storeroom containing everything required for breakfast, which important meal, in England, belongs especially to her department. . . . On the other side of this building is the washing establishment with a small courtyard attached; it consists of three rooms, the first for washing, the second for ironing, the third which is considerably loftier and heated by steam, for drying the linen in bad weather. Near the butler's room is his pantry, a spacious fire-proof room, with closets on every side for the reception of plate, which he cleans here, and the glass and china used at dinner, which must be delivered back into his custody as soon as it is washed by the women. . . . A locked staircase leads from the pantry into the beer and wine cellar, which is likewise under the butler's jurisdiction.

Many private families kept cows, to make sure of having what they considered to be unadulterated milk. The dairy was on the shady and sheltered side of the house and, we are told:

> The walls inside are usually covered with Dutch glazed tiles, the flooring also of glazed tiles, set in asphalte . . . and the ceiling lath and plaster painted . . . a thatched roof is considered most suitable . . . [it] is usually surrounded by shelves of marble or slate . . . a large table of stone in the centre, with a water-tight ledge all round it, in which water may remain in hot weather. Double windows are recommended, of the lattice kind, so that they may open, and with wire gauze blinds, and calico blinds which may be wetted when additional coolness is required. . . .

The dairy utensils needed were churns, milk-pails for each cow, hair sieves, slices of tin, milk-pans, marble dishes for cream, scales and weights, wooden bowls, butter-moulds and butter-patters, wooden tubs for washing the utensils and a portable rack for drying them.

One recipe book suggests that in winter, when the milk is white and 'tallowy' in colour because the cows are fed in stalls, the dairymaid should colour the milk for table use, 'by scraping a red carrot into a clean piece of linen cloth, dipping it into water, and squeezing it into the milk'!

In a country vicarage, in 1850, there were three servants living in—a cook, a house-parlour-maid and a girl. A daughter of the family wrote also of 'a widow who lived in a cottage nearby [who] came in to bake and to help when required. She always wore her bonnet and clattered about the kitchen and scullery in pattens. . . .'

The management of a household, large or small, was something that had to be learnt, then as much as now. Until the nineteenth century, cook-books were intended only for the housewife, but in 1816 *A New System of Domestic Cookery*, written 'by a lady'—who did not divulge her name—was written for servants, many of whom were by now able to read. This 'lady' goes into great detail:

> Every article should be kept in that place best suited to it, and much waste may thereby be avoided, viz. Vegetables will keep best on a stone floor if the air be excluded—meat in a cold, dry

place—sugar and sweetmeats require a dry place; so does salt. Candles cold, but not damp.

Bread is now so heavy an article of expense, that all waste should be guarded against; and having it cut in the room will tend much to prevent it. Since the scarcity of 1795 and 1800, that custom has been much adopted. It should not be cut until a day old.

Straw to lay apples on should be quite dry; large pears should be tied up by the stalks. . . .

The cook should be encouraged to be careful of coals and cinders; for this latter there is a new contrivance to sift, without dispersing the dust of the ashes, by means of a covered tin bucket.

In 1802 an Exeter iron-founder, George Bodley, patented a closed-top cooking range, which was the prototype of all later kitchen ranges. The front of the fire was still open for roasting, there was a fire-brick on the fire side of the oven, which prevented the food inside from scorching, and an iron flue extended up the chimney.

Closed ranges of this type were soon very popular and gradually became standard equipment in new houses. They were used a great deal in Devonshire, because the roomy hot-plate was useful for scalding pans of milk in cream-making. Bricked-in units were called 'kitchen ranges', while a 'portable range', or 'kitchener', which was an American type, stood on four legs and had an iron flue. Most ranges generated a great deal of smoke and soot, had to be blackleaded and brushed daily, and consumed an extravagant amount of coal. In many cottage homes cooking was still done over an open down-hearth.

A cookery book published in Vermont in 1845 describes the rough and ready method by which women had to regulate the heat of their oven before the era of automatic controls:

For pies, cakes, and white bread the heat of the oven should be such that you can hold your hand and arm while you count 40; for brown bread, meats, beans, Indian puddings and pumpkin pies, it should be hotter, so that you can only hold it in while you count 20.

In 1842 a book entitled *The English Housekeeper, or Manual of Domestic Management* had this to say about the new kind of kitchen fire:

I know of no apparatus so desirable as the common kitchen range, that which has a boiler for hot water, on one side, and an oven on the other side . . . there is a great difference in the construction of these little ovens. We have had several, and only three which answered. . . . The Jack is an article of great consequence, and also a troublesome one, being frequently out of repair. A Bottle-jack answers very well for a small family; and where there is a good meat screen, which is indispensable, a stout nail and a skein of worsted will, provided the cook be not called away from the kitchen, be found to answer the purpose of a spit.

But the author pointed out a snag in connection with another piece of equipment:

A clock, in or near the kitchen will tend to promote punctuality. But the lady herself should see to its being regulated, or this piece of furniture may do more harm than good. There is nothing fitter to be under lock and key than the clock; for however true to time, when not interfered with, it is often made to bear false testimony. That good understanding which sometimes subsists between the clock and the cook, and which is brought about by the instrumentality of a broom-handle, or some such magic, should be noted by every prudent housekeeper as one of the things to be guarded against.

The Industrial Revolution was, during most of the nineteenth century, producing innumerable new domestic products and objects which had to be brought to the notice of potential female customers. In

43 Mangle, 1850

1859 Mr Sam Beeton, a publisher, produced a magazine, *The English-woman's Domestic Magazine*, tuned to the rising literacy of women and their widening horizons. It dealt with cooking, washing, bringing up children, dress-making and flower-arrangement, and was the first magazine to offer its readers paper patterns of garments. The reader had to write to the editor, enclosing forty-two postage stamps, which procured a great novelty—'a full size pattern, tacked together and trimmed'.

Mr Beeton's wife, Isabella, wrote monthly supplements for this magazine, and these became a highly popular serial. The complete set of articles, 'handsomely and strongly bound in cloth', as Mr Beeton advertised it, was published in 1861 and since that date 'Mrs Beeton's' has been the guide, philosopher and friend of countless households.

Beeton's Book of Household Management is indeed an unrivalled guide to the manners and attitudes of the Victorian housewife. It seems strange to us, nowadays, that the author should have thought it important to decree 'the following scale of servants suited to various incomes':

About £1,000 a year—Cook, upper and under housemaid, man servant.
About £750 a year—Cook, housemaid and man servant.
About £500 a year—Cook, housemaid and foot-boy.
About £300 a year—Cook and housemaid.
About £200 or £150 a year—General Servant or girl for rough work.

and she added:

If there be any children, where the income will allow of it, nurses will be required in addition to the servants named. In the case of very moderate incomes a nurse sometimes combines the duties of housemaid if there are not many children, while in other cases it is necessary to keep a nurse instead of a housemaid, and let the plain cook be a general servant.

It does not seem that there is any more of a 'rat race' in our day than there was a hundred years ago!

Mrs Beeton's advice to the mistress of a large household includes a table of wages for domestics, listing men and women separately 'in the order in which they are usually ranked'. The female servants were:

	When no extra allowance is made for tea, sugar and beer	When an extra allowance is made for tea, sugar and beer
	£ £	£ £
The Housekeeper	From 20 to 45	From 18 to 40
The Lady's Maid	12 to 25	10 to 20
The Head Nurse	15 to 30	13 to 26
The Cook	14 to 30	12 to 26
The Upper Housemaid	12 to 20	10 to 17

The Upper Laundry-maid	12 to 18	1c to 15
The Maid-of-all-work	9 to 14	7½ to 11
The Under Housemaid	8 to 12	6½ to 10
The Still-room Maid	9 to 14	8 to 12
The Nursemaid	8 to 12	5 to 10
The Under Laundry-maid	9 to 14	8 to 12
The Kitchen-maid	9 to 14	8 to 12
The Scullery-maid	5 to 9	4 to 8

It was easy to get servants, because there were only four sources of employment for women—as a governess or lady's companion for the genteel, in domestic service for a women or girl with a 'character', and in prostitution for the rest. And, in any case, girls in service were usually much better off than they would be in a poor home. Wages were low, families were large and thousands of homes were cramped for space and desperately short of money. A mother was thankful to get 'a good place' for a daughter when she left school at the age of twelve, if, in fact, she went to school at all before the Forster Education Act of 1870 made it compulsory for her to do so.

In the country servants could still be hired at the mop fair. This was a statute fair, held after Michaelmas, and had become a kind of servants' carnival. There were 'servants' registration societies' in many towns, but the mop fair was still the popular way of finding a job, it was the only holiday most servants ever had. At the mop fair the market place would be filled with stalls, the public houses filled with customers, and by the side of the market place the servants stood in rows, most of them displaying a traditional sign to indicate their particular abilities. The shepherds held their crooks and put a piece of wool under the bands of their beaver hats; the cowherds and ploughmen carried a piece of cowhair; the waggoners had a piece of twisted silk whipcord. Servants had traditionally carried brushes, brooms or mops.

These recollections of a girl who started life as a scullery maid show that it was very hard. Such a girl was often, and for good reason, called a 'slavey':

I went as a between-maid to the Big House when I left school— six in the morning to mostly eleven at night. All the vegetables, and the washing up used to come out about half-past three, and then it was all mine. . . . Cook was a real old tartar . . . a tweeny was nobody and got nobody's rations, and no time to eat them anyway. All the maids' rooms to sweep out and dust, and the attic passage to scrub every week . . . flagstones as wide as this room and the whole length of the house . . . I only had free from four o'clock on a Sunday. I used to run home two miles for a cup of tea, and then Mother would walk back with

me sometimes—or more often run, so I wouldn't be late for
servants' church at six.

Most employers sent their servants to 'servants' church' because
a cold supper was usual on Sunday evening. Morning church for the
servants would have been inconvenient because the family preferred to
have a hot Sunday lunch. The convenience of employees was only rarely
considered; indeed, they were an entirely separate race of people, who
rarely had any real contact with their 'betters'. A Victorian precept
underlined the distinction thus: 'Servants talk about People; Gentlefolk
discuss Things.'

Mrs Beeton ruled that 'Deference to a master and mistress, and
to their friends and visitors, is one of the implied terms of [a servant's]
engagement. . . . A servant is not to be seated, or wear a hat in the
house, in his master's or mistress's presence; nor offer any opinion,
unless asked for it; nor even to say "good night" or "good morning",
except in reply to that salutation.'

Early rising was, to her, a cardinal virtue, in a mistress as in a
servant, but 'early' had a different meaning for each:

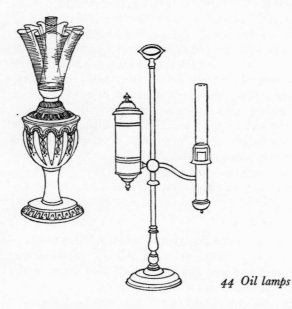

44 Oil lamps

The housemaid who studies her own ease will certainly be at
her work by six o'clock in the summer, and probably half past
six or seven in the winter months, having spent a reasonable
time in her own chamber in dressing. Earlier than this would
probably be an unnecessary waste of coals and candle in winter.

Not, we note, an unnecessary waste of effort for the poor housemaid!

The housemaid's duties were more general than those of other servants, and from the paragraphs dealing with her work, we catch a glimpse of many small domestic details which seem far more than a century away from our day.

In the rooms which she 'does' before breakfast, she must lay a cloth of coarse wrapping in front of the stove, and on it place her housemaid's box containing black-lead brushes, leathers, emery-paper, cloth, black-lead, and her cinder-pail. . . . Some mistresses, to save labour, have a double set of fire-bars, one bright set for the summer, and another black set to use when the fires are in use. . . . Before sweeping the carpets she sprinkles them all over with tea leaves, 'to give a slightly fragrant smell to the room' (of course all the carpets, like the rest of the décor, were in dark colours). . . . Before laying the cloth for breakfast, the heater of the tea-urn is to be placed in the hottest part of the kitchen fire. . . . She takes the breakfast-cloth from the napkin press. . . .

Already the poor girl must feel worn out but—'Breakfast served, the housemaid proceeds to the bed-chambers. . . .' She empties and washes the basin and ewers, empties the slops, and washes and scalds and wipes everything dry. Before beginning the bedmaking, velvet chairs should be removed to another room. The beds are, of course, feather beds, for we read that 'some like beds sloping from the top towards the feet, swelling slightly in the middle, others, perfectly flat; a good housemaid will accommodate each bed to the taste of the sleeper, taking care to shake, beat and turn it well in the process'. Any feathers which escape should be put back through the seam of the tick and 'she will also be careful to sew up any stitch that gives way the moment it is discovered'. After the bed is made the bed-curtains are drawn to the

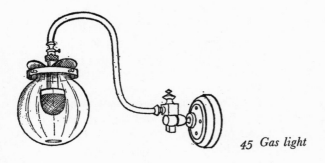

45 Gas light

head and folded neatly across the bed. . . . Once a week, when a bedroom is to be thoroughly cleaned . . . she should shake the bed curtains, lay them smoothly on the bed, pin up the valance, so that she can sweep under the bed . . . unloop the window-curtains and pin them high up out of the way . . . sprinkle the carpet with a little freshly-pulled grass when available. . . . Bedroom floors must be scrubbed but in the winter (we are relieved to read) 'it is not advisable to scrub rooms too often, as nothing is more dangerous than to allow persons to sleep in a damp room. . . .'

The housemaid also waits at table, 'her dress made with closed sleeves' so that they do not fall into any of the food. She should not wear creaking boots when waiting, but should move about as noiselessly as possible. Dinner over, she brushes off the crumbs with a curved crumb-brush into the hand-tray kept for that purpose. But her duties are not finished yet, for during winter fires must be lit in the dressing rooms an hour before the usual time of retiring, placing a fire-guard before each fire, and the night-things on the horse should be placed before the fire to be aired, with a tin can of hot water 'if the mistress is in the habit of washing before going to bed'!

If all this were not enough, Mrs Beeton suggests that 'on leisure days, the housemaid should be able to do some needlework for her mistress, such as turning and mending sheets and darning the house linen'. And, so that no time is ever spent idle, she adds 'Useful Recipes for Housemaids'—how to clean marble, to clean floorcloth (wet it all over with milk and rub with a dry cloth), to clean decanters, to brighten gilt frames and how to preserve fire-irons from rust.

In the 1880s, the author of *The Management of Servants: a Practical Guide to the Routine of Domestic Service* describes the duties of a cook in a small household, and we feel breathless with her efforts:

A plain cook in a small household where no kitchen or scullery maid is kept, and where the work of the house is done by a housemaid who also acts as parlourmaid . . . is expected to be down at six in the summer and half-past six in the winter, and she lights the kitchen fire and gets through her work upstairs before putting her kitchen in order; then she lays the kitchen breakfast for the family, she assists the housemaid to make her mistress's bed, and she answers the door up to half-past twelve. Plain cooking makes but very little work in comparison with professed cooking. . . . The dinner generally consists of fish, a joint and vegetables, a pudding or tart; and the luncheon is either a joint, vegetables and plain pudding, or cold meat, salad and potatoes. . . . A hot joint for luncheon, with vegetables . . . answers for luncheon in the dining-room, for the children's dinner, and for the servants' dinner.
The early part of the afternoon is required for scullery work. She has then to prepare the dining-room dinner, which is served either at half-past six or seven. [She] has the scullery

work to do after the dinner is sent up, and to lay the supper-table for the servants' supper in the kitchen, and afterwards to clear it away. . . . It is also her duty to see that the doors and windows of the basement are fastened securely, that the kitchen fire has burnt low, and that the gas in the kitchen and passages is turned off before retiring for the night, from ten to half-past ten.

The Victorian breakfast was usually at eight o'clock, followed by family prayers, an occasion attended by family, visitors and servants alike. Even this required the services of a domestic, as was described by the vicar's daughter:

When my father was old he went to sleep while reading family prayers and my mother had to wake him and then sometimes he began all over again, so that prayers were very long, or he skipped a page so that they were very short. The parlour-maid used to bring in the large Prayer-Book on a silver salver and say 'Prayers are on the table, sir.'

Many poor families were living in great misery throughout the nineteenth century and some recipe books had a special section on 'Cookery for the Poor'—'some recipes which may, perhaps, be of use to young housekeepers who are actuated by the benevolent desire of contributing to the comfort of their poor neighbours'.

Mrs Beeton had advice to give about this matter also:

Great advantages may result from visits paid to the poor; for there being, unfortunately, much ignorance, generally, amongst them with respect to all household knowledge, there will be opportunities for advising and instructing them, in a pleasant and unobtrusive manner, in cleanliness, industry, cookery, and good management.

It is easy for us to scoff at this, but there was real kindness, much charity—in the true sense of the word—and great social responsibility among the Victorians.

The public conscience was much troubled by the dreadful housing conditions in the new industrial towns in the north. One Government report referred to the struggle which even the most careful housewife had, to keep her family decent in the new back-to-back houses:

It was often affecting . . . to see the floors of their houses and the steps washed clean and made white with the hearthstone . . . to see their clothes washed and hung out to dry, but befouled by soot from the neighbouring furnaces. . . .

But only very few of the poor managed to rise above their dreadful domestic circumstances. In overcrowded courts, alleys and back-streets there was virtually no sanitation and often the only water supply was a pump or a standpipe a long way off. The wretched homes were overcrowded and it was not uncommon for seven or eight people to live in one or two rooms, without a kitchen of any kind whatever.

Not that many of the women had any idea of what good house-keeping was. They had not been in service in good households as country girls had, and most of them had not been taught to cook, to clean, or to bring up children. In particular their extravagance in buy-ing and using food was often deplored by the middle classes.

The living conditions of cottagers were often no better, but they, at least, often had a patch of garden and the countryside near at hand. Many a family lived, ate and slept in one room; cooking, washing, iron-ing, mending, all had to be done there or, perhaps, in a lean-to wash-house. Water had to be carried in pails from a well, pump or river, and few cottagers had a sink or a water butt.

But in a child's book of 1837 we read of happier conditions at harvest time—at least to the eye of an outside observer:

> The humblest cottager wears a smile during the happy season of harvest. Everyone that is of age to work, is then fully employed and well paid. Money comes in freely, and the pinch of want is not felt as at other times in the dwellings of the poor. At the first gleam of early sunshine, the industrious peasant, with such of his sons as are able to assist in his labours, goes forth, carrying in his scrip, or bag, a portion of food sufficient for the day. At eight o'clock, his careful wife, after giving her family their breakfast, leads out her little train to glean, leaving her eldest girl to keep house, nurse the babe, and take care of any of the children who are too young to glean. She has also to scrub or sweep the floor, and cook the supper against the return of the family. The supper, which is always the principal meal, generally consists of hard flour-dumplings, with vegetables, and sometimes, as in harvest-time, a morsel of meat, and a drop of gravy by way of sauce. I am always delighted, when returning from my evening walks, to peep into the cottages of the Suffolk peasants, and see the various members of families collecting in smiling groups round a cleanly but humble board, and enjoying the pleasure of an affectionate re-union at the evening meal. On one occasion, I observed a table neatly spread outside the cottage door, and the good man and his family supping in the open air, under the loaded branches of a fine apple tree.

This description of a Harvest Home describes the festivity at the end of everyone's labours:

> [In the best kitchen] there was Mrs Elsmore herself, armed with

her large bunch of keys, of which she seemed always to be selecting one for especial use; and then there was someone always chopping or beating eggs; and another always moving some kettle or saucepan on the hearth; and there was a constant noise of the smoke-jack in the wide chimney, under the pressure of a tremendous piece of beef, which caused every black wheel in the higher regions to utter sounds not unlike the skirlings of an ill-conditioned pipe. The very dogs seemed to be on the alert, and from always being in the way, received many a kick, which sent them yelping into other parts of the busy scene. And as the hours advanced, and the report arrived from the fields respecting the progress of the work in that quarter, the fervour of preparation in the kitchen became hotter, and the old and the young ran faster and got more and more into each other's way, till at length Mrs Elsmore, coming to a stand in the very middle of the kitchen, gave one scientific glance around her, and exclaimed: 'They may come now as soon as they will; if nothing has been forgotten, we are all ready.'

Irish peasants had always been poor, and when the potato crop failed during successive years in the middle of the century, famine was widespread, whole families starved and many thousands died. In some towns soup-kitchens were set up, where the people could get a ration of bread and hot soup in exchange for special coupons issued to the most needy. Posters were printed in Ireland, showing the plenty that was available in the United States, and large numbers of families emigrated.

Desperate poverty continued in spite of humanitarian attempts of help, but by the closing years of the century many skilled workers were living fairly comfortably, as was shown in a report on *The Conditions of the Wage-Earning Classes in York* which described the kitchens thus:

The houses usually contain five rooms and a scullery. . . . The real living-room is the kitchen, rendered cheerful and homely by the large open grate and the good oven, unknown in the south, but familiar in the north of England where coal is cheap, and where the thrifty housewife bakes her own bread. The floor of this room is commonly covered with linoleum, though a large home-made hearthrug may lend an air of solid comfort. A sofa, albeit of horsehair or American cloth, an arm-chair, polished tins, and china ornaments on the high mantelpiece, add the subtle touch of homeliness. Though small, the scullery, which is provided with a sink, water-tap and 'copper' for washing, contributes to the comfort of the house.

The domestic water supply in most towns was still very irregular, and even in some well-to-do areas at the beginning of the century it was only available three times a week. When running water became freely available it seldom supplied any part of the house except the basement. It served the kitchen sink, but the servants had to carry it upstairs for other uses. Sometimes members of a family would take a bath in the stone-floored back kitchen on Saturday night, in hot water brought from

46 Gas fire

the copper to a tin hip-bath. While there were servants in plenty to stagger up and down stairs with water-cans there was little incentive, even for those who could afford it, to go to the trouble and expense of installing piping.

Many people still considered baths to be dangerous and believed that undressing between November and March would bring on a dangerous chill. In Pennsylvania in the eighteen-forties there was an attempt to make it illegal to take a bath between those months. In 1840 some Americans denounced the bath tub as an 'epicurean innovation from England, designed to corrupt the simplicity of the Republic', and when in 1851 it was announced that a bathroom was going to be installed in the White House, a public furore arose, attacking such unnecessary expenditure!

It was not until the eighteen-fifties that gas was used for water heating, and many of the early 'geysers' were very dangerous and explosions were frequent. Gas lighting was safer, but very dirty, since unburned particles in the flame of a gas burner left dark grey shadows over the gasolier and on the walls and ceiling nearby.

It was because of the collection of soot from gas and oil lamps that the Victorian housewife embarked upon the elaborate ritual of spring-cleaning. We hear nothing of it in earlier centuries. At the end of the winter they took down the heavy winter curtains, shook them outside, brushed them, and pinned them on paper or linen, with camphor to preserve them from the moths. Draperies, carpets and upholstery had to have the loose soot beaten out of them, ceilings were washed and re-whitened, and the white summer curtains and the light chair-covers were put on.

47 *Tin hip-bath*

Such upheavals were very unwelcome, but were certainly necessary until the invention of the gas-mantle in the early eighteen-eighties, and until, much later, less crowded rooms meant that there was less likelihood of dirt collecting. The gas-mantle was a cleaner installation and a soft light, warm, murmuring and friendly, with occasional light popping as air built up in the narrow pipes.

The first appliance for cooking by gas was made in 1824, and looked rather like a gridiron with small holes in it. Frying could be done by setting the pan on the top of the gridiron, but for roasting the gridiron was set horizontally, so that the gas jets pointed towards the meat hung in front of them. A tin reflector called a 'hastener' was set behind the roast to reflect the heat.

Housewives and cooks were slow to trust this new way of cooking. In 1841, however, Alexis Soyer, the famous chef of the Reform Club in London, had gas cookers installed in the club kitchens and declared that they were an economy since they only needed to be lit when in use. What was good enough for the great Soyer was good enough for many British housewives and gas cooking gradually became accepted. A gas cooker was on view at the Great Exhibition in 1851. It was a clumsy affair with a great deal of cast-iron decoration which would collect dust and grease, but by 1870 plainer gas cookers with a number of labour-saving devices were being sold, many of them for use in American kitchens. Oil cookers were introduced in America in 1880 and soon became very popular there.

Cleaning the lights was a messy business. Even after gas was used in the main rooms of some large houses, paraffin lamps were still general.

They had wicks of cotton boiled in vinegar, and the vase holding the oil was usually of brass or earthenware. The lamps from every room in the house had to be collected each morning and filled, cleaned and trimmed. In a large house this was usually done in a special 'lamp-room', or in the back kitchen. Mrs Beeton recommended 'utmost care' in cleaning oil lamps and added 'the best mode of doing which she [the ubiquitous house-maid] will do well to learn from the tradesman who supplies the oil'.

A short cut to getting a light, in place of the time-honoured tinder-box, was the sulphur match—a splint of wood or a spill of paper coated at the end with a small quantity of yellow sulphur.

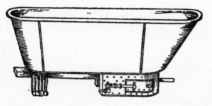

48 *Cast-iron bath*
with gas-burner underneath

In *The Tinder Box,* published in 1832, there is a description of the making of the matches which beggars used to sell on the streets. They used to beg ends of wood from carpenters' shops, cut them into slivers and dipped them into a small pot of heated brimstone. Both ends were tipped and the matches left to cool.

In most households fires were still lit with the help of a tinder-box and in a large establishment this was the responsibility of the housemaid. She dried cotton or linen rags before the fire and charred them by setting them alight and then extinguishing them with the close-fitting inside lid of the tinder-box.

The sulphur match made it easier to get a light from smouldering tinder, but to light the tinder in the first place required considerable skill. In *The Tinder Box* the author remarked that—

> You cannot have blood out of a stone, but a stone may easily
> have blood out of you. On a cold dark frosty morning when
> the hands are chapped, frozen and insensible, you may chance
> to strike the flint against the knuckles for a considerable time
> without discovering your mistake. . . . There are few house-men
> or house-maids who can succeed in striking a light in less than
> three minutes.

Gas for lighting, heating and cooking was gradually overtaken by electricity, and this had enormous effects in the kitchen. At first electricity was very expensive, but it had the advantages of requiring little servicing, and no trimming or cutting of wicks; and there was no risk of explosion. Electric ranges were made from about 1890 but they did not become popular until some thirty years later. By the end of the nineteenth-century, many manufacturers' catalogues listed and illustrated most of the electric cooking equipment that we know today: kettles, saucepans, frying-pans, toasters, roasters, hot-plates, ovens, coffee-grinders, immersion heaters and electric fans.

But even when electric gadgets were in use in some better-equipped kitchens, the bedrooms, dining-rooms, drawing-rooms, studies, libraries and nurseries were still heated (if that word can really be said to apply) by coal fires. In summer the yawning iron grates were furnished with 'summer ornaments' and, says Mrs Beeton:

> We know none prettier than the following, which the house-maid may provide at a small expense to her mistress:–
> Purchase two yards and a half of crinoline muslin, and tear it into small strips, the selvage way of the material, about an inch wide; strip this thread by thread on each side, leaving the four centre threads; this gives about six and thirty pieces, fringed on each side, which are tied together at one end, and fastened to the trap of the register, while the threads, unravelled, are spread gracefully about the grate, the lower part of which is filled with paper shavings. This makes a very elegant and very cheap ornament, which is much stronger, besides, than those usually purchased.

What a perfect example of the transience of 'elegance'!

Cleaning the table silver was a weekly job in all but the poorest households. Hartshorn powder, ground—but not at home—from the shavings of deer's antlers, was made into a thick paste with spirits of wine, left on the plate for some time and then brushed off and polished with special plate-rags. These were made 'from the tops of old cotton stockings' boiled in a mixture of new milk and hartshorn powder, in the proportion of 1 oz of powder to 1 pint of milk, boiled for five minutes and dried before the fire.

Knife-cleaning machines made by Kent, or Masters, were rapidly taking the place of the earlier knife-board. Such a machine had a drum-shaped wooden casing, into which the knives were inserted through holes in the edge, and a handle turned a series of brushes inside. Small and large machines were made, some cleaning only four knives, while others cleaned as many as twelve at once.

Floor polish had to be made, from candle ends, beeswax and turpentine and a recipe for boot polish is described as 'never so good as . . . can be made after the following recipe':

Take of ivory-black and treacle each 4 oz, sulphuric acid 1 oz, neat olive-oil 2 spoonfuls, best white-wine vinegar 3 half-pints: mix the ivory-black and treacle well in an earthen jar; then add the sulphuric acid, continuing to stir the mixture; next pour in the oil; and, lastly, add the vinegar, stirring it in by degrees, until thoroughly incorporated.

Another recipe for a 'very superior polishing paste for boots and shoes' includes 3 lb of red French wine (ordinaire) and 3 lb of brandy!

It is an indication of the rising standards of living in modest homes that, during the eighteen-eighties, more and more magazines were published which contained articles about domestic discipline and economy. *The Economical Housewife,* published in 1882, stressed that the cleanliness of the house depended above all on the housemaids. The writer was not in favour of employing a daily charwoman, for they were said to cost a shilling a day, drink gin, and spend most of their time gossiping!

Another article, in the same magazine, gave careful directions for the weekly turning out of rooms and the extermination of fleas, flies and bugs in the beds. Bedsteads should be taken to pieces and thoroughly washed every year.

In large towns the laundry of wealthy families was by now sent out to professional laundresses or to one of the new 'laundry companies'. But the chemical processes which they employed were said to injure fabrics and in many households the fine linen, cottons and muslins, were washed and 'got-up' at home, even where the bulk of the washing was given out. In suburban and country homes washing was always done at home.

The laundry establishment of a sizeable country household consisted of a washing-house, an ironing and drying-room, and sometimes a drying-closet heated by furnaces. The washing-house was usually attached to the kitchen, with a York-stone floor laid on brick piers, and sloping gently towards a gutter connected with the drain. A range of wooden tubs with hot and cold taps and a boiler and furnace were all the equipment of this room.

The adjoining bleaching-house contained a mangle, clothes-horses for drying and airing, a large deal table for ironing, with drawers for ironing-blankets, a hot-plate built into the chimney, with a furnace underneath it for heating the irons.

A family wash was still a complicated event. In many households the coppers had to be heated by one or two o'clock in the morning; other domestic work was put aside for a day or two, and extra help was hired to help the maids.

In the country, washing was followed by rinsing and beating in running water and bleaching on grass. This last process was called 'bucking'. Most households had a set of 'tenterhooks', on which woollen goods were stretched to dry. Tenter-poles were like football posts, with iron hooks along the top and sides, and a log of heavy wood that hung loose and fastened on to the bottom of the cloth. It was 'on tenterhooks' while drying and so did not need any pressing.

Silk handkerchiefs had to be washed alone and soaked well when they contained snuff.

Mrs Beeton goes into great detail about various kinds of irons, and one cannot help wondering to whom she thought it necessary to describe them. There can surely never have been a wife or maid, however young, who had not seen ironing done in these ways but to us the description comes as if from another world:

> The irons consist of the common flat-iron, which is of different sizes, varying from 4 to 10 inches in length, triangular in form, and from $2\frac{1}{2}$ to $4\frac{1}{2}$ inches in width at the broad end; the oval iron, which is used for more delicate articles; and the box-iron, which is hollow and heated by a red-hot iron inserted into the box. The Italian iron is a hollow tube, smooth on the outside, and raised on a slender pedestal with a footstalk. Into the hollow cylinder a red-hot iron is pushed which heats it; and the smooth outside of the latter is used, on which articles such as frills, and plaited articles, are drawn. Crimping and gauffering-machines are used for a kind of plaiting where much regularity is required, the articles being passed through two iron rollers fluted so as to represent the kind of plait or fold required.

If one of the many irons she used should scorch the linen, the colour could be restored by using the following recipe:

> $\frac{1}{2}$ pint of vinegar, 2 oz of fuller's earth, 1 oz of dried fowls' dung, $\frac{1}{2}$ oz of soap, the juice of 2 large onions. Boil all these ingredients together to the consistency of paste; spread the composition thickly over the damaged part, and if the threads be not actually consumed, after it has been allowed to dry on, and the place has subsequently been washed once or twice, every trace of scorching will disappear.

China was still a cherished possession. The lady of the house often washed it up herself and put it back into the special china cupboard in the breakfast room. Enamel ware was much used in kitchens early in the century; it was called 'Japan ware' because it was made of tin washed over with a transparent brown varnish, resembling oriental lacquer.

In those families where there were many servants, women and girls sometimes had time to kill and they spent a good deal of it in doing embroidery of various kinds. Cushion-covers had to be made, and covers for mantelpieces, tables, footstools and dressing-tables. 'Berlin' woolwork was popular in England—presumably owing to the influence of the Prince Consort—and patchwork in the United States. Most girls in both countries were expected to sew a sampler, a piece of canvas on which stitches were practised and then an uplifting text sewn. And 'an active and bustling servant girl', so the indefatigable Mrs Beeton tells us, 'will always find time to do a little needlework for herself. . . . In the summer evenings she should manage to sit down for two or three hours, and for a short time in the afternoons in leisure days'.

Until the coming of the railways in the first half of the nineteenth century, the country housewife was faced with the same difficulties and the same anxieties about her domestic supplies as her predecessors had been. She grew what she could, and had to make a special journey, perhaps once a quarter, to buy other supplies in the nearest market town. But the 'iron horse' distributed goods widely and quickly and made catering much easier; there was a great impetus given to the use of fish, for example, and Victorian cookery books describe a wide variety of recipes for fish dishes. Mrs Beeton gives advice about marketing this, that and the other, and seems to have taken it for granted that the readers would be able to buy everything they needed. In her books nobody grows food, hunts it, or makes it; she is the first townswoman's cookery adviser.

The range of fruit and vegetables available to the town housekeeper was considerable. Most was still grown in Britain, but increasing amounts came from abroad, from places as far afield as America. William Hone's *The Table Book,* published in 1898, refers to grapes being available from the middle of June to the middle of November, 'but dear'; cherries were the Bigarreau or Graffion and also the black or Dutch Guigne; pears were English Jargonelle, Windsor and Green Chisel; apples were mainly Dutch Codlin, Carlisle Codlin, Jenneting, Summer Pearmain and Hawthornden. Watercress and most of the herbs sold in Covent Garden were supplied by women who gathered them wild in the countryside. Dandelions, scurvy-grass, bittersweet, feverfew, red valerian, and hedge mustard were still available for kitchen use.

Prunes and other dried fruit have been imported into Britain since the Middle Ages. The ancestral home of the plum is the Middle East, but the connection is only retained in the name 'damson', a corruption of Damascene, meaning of or from Damascus. At Christmas time, in the nineteenth century, prunes were put into plum porridge, the ancestor of Christmas pudding, a mixture of tongue, suet, raisins, spices, wine and breadcrumbs which had been popular in the seventeenth century.

Plum pudding and mixtures of meat and sugar were traditionally eaten at harvest time. Reapers were hired for a month, and if the farmer did not provide a good plum pudding for the men, to follow pickled pork and boiled beef, he was liable to find it difficult to hire good reapers the following year.

The tomato was for a long time regarded with suspicion, as not being 'wholesome'. Cooks were undecided whether to treat it as a fruit or a vegetable, and until the middle of the nineteenth century it did not figure prominently in recipes.

An Italian who visited England early in the century is remembered only for his remark about England being a country of sixty religions and only one sauce. But he was confusing two very different things: then, as now, English sauces were 'relishes', accompaniments to a dish, whereas in France a sauce is an essential ingredient of the dish whose method of cooking it implies. Another distinction is that English sauces are mainly based on vinegar, not on butter or cream as in France. The name 'chutney' is Indian in origin and 'ketchup' is said to come from the Chinese word for the brine of pickled fish.

The East India Company had a wide influence in introducing Eastern dishes to England. Many people who had lived and traded in India became accustomed to spicy, highly seasoned food and on their return home brought the tradition with them. It became smart to serve Eastern types of food.

Most English sauces started in the domestic kitchen, but many of them were commercially produced by this time. The earliest sauces were called after their originators—Harvey's and Burgess's chief among them. In an advertisement in *The Times* of 1788 a Mr Burgess had announced that he could supply, from his address in the Strand, London, where he traded as an 'Oilman and Italian Warehouseman', the following among other odd-sounding commodities:

Newfoundland Cod's Sound, Rein Deer Tongues, Bologna Sausages, Superfine Sallard Oil, Zoobditty Mutch and Hambro' Sour Croat.

During the nineteenth century 'store sauces', which had originally meant sauces made at home for the store cupboard, came to mean sauces bought in a store. Lazy cookery had started.

The practice of home brewing also began to die out at this time. William Cobbett, that tireless chronicler of the English countryside, wrote in 1821:

To show Englishmen, forty years ago, that it was good for them to brew beer in their houses, would have been as impertinent as to gravely insist that they ought to endeavour not to lose their breath; for in those times, to have a *house* and not to brew was a rare thing indeed. Mr Ellman, an old man and a large farmer in Sussex, has recently given, in evidence before the House of Commons, this fact: That forty years ago there was not a labourer in his parish that did not brew his own beer; and that now there is not one that does it, except by chance that the malt be given to him.

Beer had hitherto been the drink of the poorer classes, but during the nineteenth century it became accepted at all levels of society. An interesting sidelight on the eating and drinking habits of her time is given by Mrs Beeton, in her directions for a successful picnic party (of forty people):

A joint of cold roast beef, a joint of cold boiled beef, 2 ribs of lamb, 2 shoulders of lamb, 4 roast fowls, 2 roast ducks, 1 ham, 6 medium sized lobsters, 1 piece of collared calves head, 18 lettuces, 6 baskets of salad, 6 cucumbers, stewed fruit well sweetened and put into glass bottles well corked, 3 or 4 dozen plain pastry biscuits to eat with the stewed fruit, 2 dozen fruit turnovers, 4 dozen cheese cakes, 2 cold cabinet puddings in moulds, a few jam puffs, a large cold Christmas pudding, a few baskets of fresh fruit, 3 dozen plain biscuits, a piece of cheese, 6 lbs of butter, 4 quartern loaves of household bread, 3 dozen rolls, 6 loaves of thin bread (for tea), 2 plain plum cakes, 2 pound cakes, 2 sponge cakes, a tin of mixed biscuits, $\frac{1}{2}$ lb. of tea, coffee is not suitable for a picnic, being difficult to make.

Drink was on an equally lavish scale, almost unbelievably:

3 dozen quart bottles of ale, packed in hampers, ginger beer, soda water and lemonade, of each 2 dozen bottles, 6 bottles of sherry, 6 bottles of claret, Champagne at discretion, and any other light wine that might be preferred, and two bottles of brandy.

There were no laws about keeping food fresh and between 1800 and 1850 much of the food sold was often seriously adulterated. Alum was put into bread to whiten it, lead into cider and wine, plaster of Paris into flour, chalk into milk and so on. As a result of protests by doctors and the public, the first Food and Drugs Act was passed in 1860. This authorized county authorities to appoint analysts to control the quality of foodstuffs; but there was much corruption and little interest in furthering the interests of those who wanted purer food.

Consumer interests began to make themselves heard with greater emphasis and as a result a further act was passed in 1872, compelling the appointment of public analysts and shop inspectors. Matters gradually improved, though an astonishing note appeared in *The Chemist and Druggist* on January 15th 1876:

> Reclaiming butter
> A startling report has been published by the *Glasgow News*, disclosing some almost incredible facts in relation to the butter trade. The journal named met with a trade circular, some time back, issued to reclaim old butter, removing any taste of tallow, grease, and also bad smells etc, at the same time slightly increasing the weight, at the rate of 7s. 6d. per cwt, if in casks, or 10s. 6d. cwt if in Irish lumps. 'Any kind of old butter out of condition', said the circular, 'and heated qualities made suitable for table use again, and it becomes quite firm.'

Even the most cynical or dispirited housewife would surely agree that matters have improved in this particular!

Looking after children does not fall strictly into the realm of the kitchen, though in modest households the young have always taken up a great deal of their mother's time, and been quite literally 'under her feet' while she was busy with domestic work.

In well-to-do families a wet-nurse was often employed, a local woman or a servant of the household who undertook to nurse other women's babies in addition to her own.

Today's mothers appreciate today's methods of cooking, straining and canning baby-foods, not only because they are more hygienic, but because they take up so much less time than the preparation of earlier foods. A hundred-year-old recipe for 'an excellent food' recommended by an American doctor for babies from three months old gives an idea of the amount of work that used to be involved in preparing one meal:

> Take about one pound of the best wheat flour, tie it tightly in a muslin bag, and boil it continuously for twelve hours; remove it from the water, allow it to cool. When required for use, grate down about two teaspoonsful into a fine powder; mix the grated flour with half a pint of tepid water; boil it a few minutes; cool it to blood heat; then mix with the gruel thus prepared the white of one small hen's egg, or the half, if it be a large one; sweeten slightly and feed the mixture to the infant.

Such slow cooking was standard practice in the kitchen of our great-grandmothers. An old New England recipe for apple-butter contained the instruction: 'stir continuously for about seven hours'! Obviously no woman could do that on her own so apple-butter-making became a festive group activity, and similarly a woman's babies probably lightened rather than increased her work in the home, since everyone would enjoy taking turns in stirring or sieving the infant's gruel.

In comfortable families a nanny looked after the children, but the cook had to provide their food and there was always trouble between nursery and kitchen. Nursery meals were at a different time from dining-room meals, nanny was fussy about what her young charges could or should eat, and in any case the servants resented having to take trays upstairs and wait on someone who—so they felt—was only a servant herself.

The principle of refrigeration was discovered in the middle of the century and was to have an enormous influence on the eating habits of both rich and poor. No longer were women as tied to their kitchen as they had previously been, and no longer were supplies as seasonally variable as before. The first cargo of frozen meat was brought from Australia in 1880 and by the end of the century frozen mutton was being imported from New Zealand as well as chilled beef from Argentina and the United States. So 'ice-houses' were no longer a necessity in the gardens of English country houses.

It was a long time before more than a very few English kitchens had domestic refrigeration. At first the kitchen refrigerator was a lidless box containing a lump of ice; later it had a closed top and a compartment for the ice. As the ice melted, the water filtered under the bottom of the food container and into a pan underneath. The first practical storage refrigerator was marketed in the 1880s.

The idea of preserving food in a vacuum dates from the eighteenth century, but it was 1810 before a patent for the process was registered in London. The inventor of the tin can, in 1813, was an American, Thomas Kensitt. Tinned meat from Australia was displayed at the Great Exhibition of 1851; it was unappetising stuff at first, but became popular with the poor as it was cheap. The industry was very slow to develop in England, but American housewives were much more enthusiastic.

Domestic life in the United States of course varied greatly from district to district. Here is what one writer tells us of the kitchen in his grandfather's home in New England in the eighteen-thirties:

Ranges must have come in before Gramp was very old, but during his boyhood the fireplace was the main thing in the kitchen. Of course there was a crane to hang kettles on. The brass kettles, of various sizes, was kind of dress-up kettles; the iron kettles were the everyday ones. They had legs, so they would either set on the hearth next to the fire, or hang by a pothook on the crane. The frying pan was more or less like a warming pan except that it was iron, with an iron cover that could be fitted on it, and an iron handle about three feet long, so that you could fish it out of the fire. There wasn't too much stuff fried then, though. Things were mostly either cooked on a spit or in a pot.

There was no baker in 'Gramp's' village; each family baked its own bread, cakes and pies, and made butter, cheese, candles and soap. There were no servants in North American homes; every member of the family helped in the work:

We raised our own flax, retted it, hackled it, dressed it and spun it . . . the wool was also spun in the family, partly by my sisters . . . the knitting of stockings was performed by the female part of the family in the evening, and especially at tea parties.

Carpets, too, were made at home in the households of New England; the warp was often of woollen yarn and the weft of odd bits of cloth cut into strips and sewed together at the ends. Quilts were made of pieces of waste calico, sewed together in octagons and quilted in rectangles. 'Quilting parties' were popular, where the women of the neighbourhood gathered to stitch, talk and take tea. In the evenings their menfolk were admitted too.

Even in cities most families continued to have the kind of kitchen which their parents and grandparents had had. An American writer who lived in New York late in the century described the kitchen of the narrow old family house, four storeys high:

The large brick-floored kitchen was really the heart of the house. There was an enormous coal stove set back into the chimney wall, with a six-foot hearthstone in front of it. The gray stone laundry tubs stood along the opposite wall, and on laundry days not much cooking was done because the copper clothes boiler was steaming on the stove all day, with the laundress trotting back and forth from the tubs to the boiler, fishing the boiled laundry out of the bubbling water with a long 'clothes stick' which had become soft and soggy from the constant hot water dips. . . . We waited for the lamplighter to come by with his long lighting stick and, with a quick touch of the flaming tip, light up the gas mantle on the lamp post at the corner.

In 1869 an American domestic reformer, Catherine Beecher, wrote a revolutionary book, *The American Woman's Home,* which proposed plans for kitchen services which still sound modern over a hundred years afterwards. Miss Beecher introduced, for the first time, the idea that the kitchen should be the core of the house, the site of a unified set of services around which the other rooms were spread. Her house was truly 'a machine for living in', though the phrase dates from a century later.

In a chapter entitled 'The Christian House', Miss Beecher analysed every cubic inch of space and organized it for a specific purpose. 'The kitchen', she wrote, 'should be like the cook's galley in a steamship, every article and utensil used in cooking for two hundred persons so arranged that with one or two steps the cook can reach all he needs.' In contrast to this idea, she described the kitchen in most large houses where 'the table furniture, the cooking materials and essentials, the sink, the eating room are at such distances apart that half the time and strength is employed in walking back and forth to collect and return the articles used'.

In Miss Beecher's view there should be built-in, classified storage areas for all household equipment and she even foresaw the need for standard sizes of cupboards, shelves, drawers and counter-tops. Part of her planned storage-space was in cupboards on rollers, which could be moved around to form screens or room-dividers, thus catering for temporary overnight visitors in a continent where hospitality was a practical necessity (see picture 56).

The kitchen floor, she says, should be covered with an oilcloth, and she explains how to obtain this:

> To procure a kitchen oilcloth as cheaply as possible, buy
> cheap tow cloth and fit it to the size and shape of the kitchen.
> Then have it stretched and nailed to the south side of the barn
> and, with a brush, cover it with a coat of thin rye paste. When
> this is dry, put on a coat of yellow paint and let it dry for a
> fortnight. Then put on a second coat . . . let it dry two months
> and it will last for many years.

Miss Beecher had much to say about sink equipment. She recommended a very novel 'grooved dish drainer' with hinges so that it either rested on the 'cook-form' or could be turned over to cover the sink. One assumes a 'cook-form' to be the framework of the sink and its surrounding cupboards (see picture 55).

Most housewives today seem to have a dish-cloth problem, and evidently this is not new. Miss Beecher instructs that three good dish-cloths, 'hemmed and finished with loops', should be hung on three separate nails over the sink; one for greasy dishes, one for dishes not greasy and one for greasy pots and kettles. 'The lady who insists upon this will not be annoyed by having her dishes washed with dark, musty and greasy rags as is too frequently the case.' A modern reader of this good advice cannot help wondering who on earth would have time to remember which cloth was which! Moreover, 'a swab, made of strips of linen tied to a stick is useful to wash nice dishes, especially small, deep articles'. And 'a soap dish with hand soap and a fork with which to use it' is also stipulated.

Pests were evidently rampant and much of the housewife's time must have been taken up with combating them:

> Bed bugs should be kept away by filling every chink in the
> bedstead with putty and painting it over.
> Flies can be killed in great quantities by placing about the
> house vessels filled with sweetened water and cobalt.
> Red and black ants may be driven away by putting Scotch
> snuff wherever they go for food.
> Against moths, if articles be tightly sewed up in linen and laid
> away, and fine tobacco put about them, in April it is a sure
> protection. . . .

Catherine Beecher was a careful housewife who believed in counting the clothes pegs and sweeping under the beds 'with short strokes'. She had a very considerate attitude to her servants and believed that success in handling them depended upon the manners of the lady of the house toward them. Severity was to be avoided at all costs: 'Few domestics, especially American domestics, will long submit to it.'

Miss Beecher wrote praisingly of the educated, hard-working women of New England in earlier days, and regretted that much of their philosophy had been lost. They were—

> handsome, strong women, rising each day to do their in-door
> work with cheerful alertness . . . and they chatted meanwhile
> of books, studies, embroidery; discussed the last new poem or
> some historical topic, or perhaps a rural ball that was to come
> off next week. They spun with the book tied to the distaff;
> they wove; they did all manner of fine needlework; they made
> lace, painted flowers. . . . A bride in those days was married
> with sheets and table-cloths of her own weaving, with counter-
> panes and toilet-covers wrought in divers embroidery by her
> own and her sisters' hands.

Miss Beecher believed in discipline, her pioneer spirit was still very strong, she knew the problems of living in a new country and wanted to help women to overcome them. A century after her book was published, many of the kitchens in the United States are direct descendants of her revolutionary ideas.

49 Early mechanical cleaner

The Twentieth Century

IN many ways the nineteenth century did not end until 1914. The Edwardian decade glowed like an autumn sunset for the many well-to-do families who still led dignified, leisured lives with an army of servants to wait upon them. They ate lavishly, entertained frequently and dressed extravagantly, yet they lived uncomfortably by our present-day standards. Rooms were cold and draughty, heated only by open fires which involved the servants in continual carrying of coals up and down stairs, and in the daily cleaning of grates.

Lady Cynthia Asquith, remembering her childhood at the beginning of the century, described another of those discomforts:

> Nor was there yet any thought of running water in the bedrooms.
> Instead, a brown-lidded can, with a turban of towel, was
> brought up morning and evening to your bedroom and placed
> on one of the two china basins on the washstand.

The servants' duties had altered little during the past fifty years and, though the décor of drawing- and dining-rooms, of bedrooms, studies and libraries had been changed as fashion changed, the kitchen quarters remained virtually the same.

The range dominated many kitchens, though in others there would be a large, clumsy gas-cooker. A huge dresser, with cupboards below, often had its shelves laden with a full dinner service of a hundred and twenty-six pieces, all of which needed to be washed once a week. The floor was usually of stone flags which needed scrubbing every day, and in the centre of the room stood a huge kitchen table which also had to be scrubbed white, with soap and soda.

Either just inside the kitchen door or in the passage outside it there was a long row of bells with indicators above them to show from which room they rang. In some large houses a system of whistles connected the various rooms to the kitchen, so that the cook, or whoever was in the kitchen when a bell rang, could whistle up to tell a servant in another room that they were wanted.

Meals were large and complicated, entertaining was on a grand scale, and so cooking was a skilled business. A kitchen-maid recalled how she had to 'lay up the cook's table' ready for preparing dinner:

> There were knives of all kinds, all shapes and sizes, big long carving knives, small knives for paring fruit, pallet knives, bent knives for scraping out basins with, metal spoons, not the ordinary type—they were like a kind of aluminium-coloured spoon—huge ones, about six of them. The largest ones had the measures on them, from ounces right up to dessertspoonfuls . . . two sieves, a hair sieve and a wire sieve, and a flour sifter and an egg whisk . . . two kinds of graters, one fine one for nutmegs, and one to do the breadcrumbs on; there was a big chopping board and a small chopping board, three or four kinds of basins, paprika pepper and cayenne pepper, ordinary salt, pepper and vinegar. Half the table was covered with these things . . . all these implements had to be laid out twice a day; for lunch, although the lunch was only three courses, and for dinner again at night, when there were five or six.

Change occurs at very different rates according to time and place. Life in a prosperous farmhouse in south Michigan at the turn of the century was still very much as it had been for a hundred years before. Their farmhouse did not have a dining-room; they ate at one end of the large kitchen. The floor was bare except for braided rugs in front of the stove and the work-table; there was a dresser, a rocking chair and an eight-day steeple clock. The cooking was done in an 'elevated oven' heated by wood; after some years it was replaced by a new-fashioned stove, with an oven below it. It is interesting to remember that the newest ovens of today are placed high on a wall, and thus have reverted to those of the nineteenth-century colonial homes.

The farmhouse kitchen was inconvenient and poorly equipped by the standards of today; it was freezing cold in winter until the morning fire was lighted, hot in summer until the stove was allowed to cool off in the afternoon, but it was homely and cheerful and very much the hub of the household.

Many of the poor in England lived in dreadful conditions, crowded eight or ten people into a room, without kitchen or washing facilities. Here is a vivid description of the derelict old house in London in which Charlie Chaplin's mother rented an attic room for herself and her two sons. No 'housekeeping' was involved in such a home and survival was all that could be aimed at:

> The house was depressing and the air foul with stale slops and old clothes. . . . Our room was stifling, a little over twelve feet square . . . the table against the wall was crowded with dirty plates and teacups; and in the corner, snug against the lower wall, was an old iron bed which Mother had painted white. Between the bed and the window was a small firegrate.

Conditions in the country were better, particularly in the North of England, where women still baked their own bread and where there was a strong sense of pride, even among quite modest families. An autobiography describes the kitchen of a farm where the author lived and worked as a boy before the First World War.

> The kitchen where we had our meals was a big, square place, with a stone-flagged floor scrubbed and scoured till it shone cold and bare as charity. A big solid-looking table stood in the centre, and here George and the missus had their meals, my seat being at the side-table near the door, which was handier for odd jobs. A stone slab with a pump stood near the window overlooking the flagged courtyard. Opposite the window was a wide fireplace with shining cooking-range, in front of which was a solitary hearthrug, the only bit of covering on that wide expanse of flags. . . . On one side of the fireplace hung a long-handled copper warming-pan, and on the other side stood a bright copper kettle, neither of which were ever used. Two brass candlesticks stood on the chimney-piece and a pair of brass snuffers hung under a cake merchant's almanack in the centre. In one corner stood a grandfather clock with a spray of roses painted across its dial. Several rows of hams and flitches [of bacon] and a double-barrelled gun, hung from the ceiling, and that was the furnishing of the great kitchen, where everything was scrubbed and scoured and uncomfortable.

The village grocer used to have to break down bulk purchases into small household portions, so buying and selling was a slow, friendly process, The sugar and oats and flour and rice were measured out of a sack, the butter cut from a block, and cheese cut in slabs from a large round ball wrapped in muslin. The shop was very much the social centre of a village.

The coming of the country bus made it possible for country women to reach a market town regularly for shopping. They had a far wider choice of goods to buy, but shopping was less personal and less individual than it had previously been. The long process had begun which has led inexorably to the supermarket and the hypermarket of our own day.

Before 1914 town housewives could buy many of the goods they needed without going to either shops or markets. There were street vendors of all kinds who went about the streets shouting or ringing a bell to attract attention. Baskets, brooms, brushes, clothes-horses and clothes-pegs were among the goods still made by hand and hawked around the streets by men, women and children carrying their wares in baskets on their heads. Fruit and vegetables were sold from large baskets, or from panniers slung on either side of a donkey, and pavement sellers offered eels, whelks, meat pies and puddings, sheep's trotters, cat and dog meat, cough drops, sweets, bread and milk. A baker's boy, dressed in white overalls, walked along crying 'Hot loaves! Hot loaves!' and during the winter afternoons the muffin man's bell announced his arrival with the trayful of muffins and crumpets which he carried on his head.

In feeding her family the housewife could now make use of more and more varied foods imported from overseas. Powdered dried milk was a great boon to mothers. This supposedly twentieth-century invention had in fact been known in the thirteenth century, but then forgotten. Marco Polo, the Venetian explorer and merchant had found that the armies of the Tartars knew how to preserve milk for use on long journeys by drying it. He said they had—

> . . . dried milk, which is solid like paste, and this is how they dry it. First they bring the milk to the boil, at the appropriate moment they skim off the cream that floats on the surface and put it into another vessel to be made into butter, they then stand the milk in the sun to leave it to dry. When they are going on a journey they take about ten pounds of this milk, and each morning take out about half a pound of it and put it in a small leather flask shaped like a gourd, with as much water as they want. While they are riding, the milk in the flask dissolves into a fluid which they drink.

From the beginning of the twentieth century there were increasing opportunities for the more intelligent girls to become shop assistants or office workers, and this led to a gradual reduction in the supply of servants. No real shortage was felt, however, until after 1914; the war brought its changes to the world of the kitchen, as elsewhere, and while the munitions factories opened their gates to women, the doors of the kitchen began to close. The number of domestic servants did not, surprisingly, increase during the depression years of the late nineteen-twenties and early nineteen-thirties. Only about five per cent of households had a resident servant at that time, and some of these were still living in basement quarters:

> . . . The so-called servants' hall, which was our sitting-room really. . . . The only light we had in our room was one bulb with a white china shade. The floor was covered in old brown lino, with horrible mis-shapen wicker chairs which had once graced their conservatory and weren't even considered good enough for that now. Depressing walls that were shiny brown paint half-way up, and a most bilious green distemper for the top half, the barred windows and one table with an old cloth . . . that was our sitting-room.

But things were changing very fast; many employers were treating their servants well, as a cook found when she changed her job in the thirties:

> It was in this house that I saw the change in the status of domestic servants. . . . In other places I'd noticed what must have been the beginnings, but here I found a complete change. Here we really counted as part of the household. . . . The kitchen was furnished with every appliance that was then known, and although it was still in the basement, it was light and airy, painted white, none of this chocolate brown half up the walls, and green the rest. In the scullery the sink was white enamel, not one of those cement affairs, and aluminium saucepans, which was a change from either iron or copper.

Hire purchase was a striking innovation in the nineteen-thirties, which had an effect upon the kitchen as well as upon other parts of the house. It enabled people without capital to buy many more household goods than they had done before, and so encouraged manufacturers to make more. Now that respectable middle-class women were having to do menial domestic tasks, there was a great demand for gadgets of all kinds. 'Labour-saving' was an expression unknown to the Victorian or Edwardian housewife, but now it became a popular concept. Previously, the kitchen was a menial area in which to work and the organizing of the household had been done from the drawing-room; now the organizer herself was finding her life centred more and more in the kitchen.

One of the changes in kitchens at this time was the conversion of the dresser, with its open shelves which collected dust, into the fitted cabinet, often with a folding or sliding enamel-topped table incorporated in the front, and with cupboards underneath or drawers lined to hold bread and flour. The 'Regulo' device for setting oven heat at a required temperature was an improvement to gas-cookers and enabled a busy housewife to get on with other work while cooking. The new 'Aga' solid-fuel, insulated cooker-heater was an invaluable innovation, though rather an expensive one. It provided a constant hot water supply, remained lit for many months without needing to be cleaned out, and was adaptable for both fast and slow cooking. Pressure-cookers, aluminium saucepans, stainless-steel cutlery and many other inventions reduced time and work in the kitchens of those who could afford them, and who were for the first time having to do their own housework.

Thought also began to be given in adapting to the kitchen such new techniques as time-and-motion study. An American expert counted the steps taken by a cook in making a cake and found that there were two hundred and eighty-one! That kitchen was re-planned and the number of steps taken was reduced to forty-five, which meant a saving of two hundred yards per cake or more than a mile to nine cakes. When we think of all the daily operations in a kitchen, this becomes a very serious matter, and there was promise of great improvements in kitchen planning when architects began to take an interest in the problem.

But families in the depressed industrial areas had a very bleak life in the two decades after the Great War. Food was largely bread and potatoes, with only occasionally a very little meat. The daughter of an unemployed cotton worker in Lancashire described conditions at home in the nineteen-twenties:

> Once a week mother queued at the butcher and came home if lucky with two pennyworth of bacon bones, and made pea-soup for midday meal for all six. . . . Hotpot and potato pie were favourite dishes. . . . Milk was delivered in a churn in a horse-trap, and ladled out of the churn into a jug with a measure. The housewife had to go out to the cart every morning and buy as much as she needed, rather than leave a standing order. . . . Newspaper was a favourite wrapping and nothing was sealed. Sugar and flour were sold loose from the sacks. Butter was cut off a huge piece (56 pounds) and slapped with butter pats. . . . Shopping was slow as everything had to be weighed. . . . Monday was washday which involved handling wet clothing from 6 a.m. to midday, washing, rinsing, blueing and starching. . . . Curtains, always two, sometimes three, lots at each window, had to be washed regularly. . . .

Although there were nearly three million unemployed in Britain during the nineteen-thirties, and nearly seven million in the United States, the P. G. Wodehouse world of Bertie Wooster and his wealthy, extravagant friends did actually exist. This description of breakfast in a large country house of the time is not exaggerated:

. . . there we really had breakfasts. There was porridge for
those who liked it. On Sundays he made waffles, with maple
syrup and pats of butter. There were eggs for boiling and a little
saucepan of hot water. There were fried and scrambled eggs,
bacon, fishcakes or kedgeree, sometimes mushrooms, sometimes
kidneys. There was a cold ham, Bradenham or Virginia. Cold
game in season, sometimes a terrine of pheasant. There were
home-made scones, a wholemeal loaf, toast; tea and coffee,
of course; honey in a comb, one or two kinds of Women's
Institute jam, marmalade. In season there were grapefruit from
Florida and sometimes pommeloes; from the garden, strawberries,
raspberries, gooseberries, currants; from the hot-house, peaches,
nectarines and grapes. A brisk walk to church and a brisk walk
back, and we were ready for a four-course luncheon.

The Second World War changed all that. Looking back at
wartime kitchens from the security and plenty of thirty years later, one
visualizes them as dreary places. Food was rationed from January 1940
and by the summer of 1941 the weekly allowances for adults were four
ounces of bacon or ham, eight ounces of sugar, two ounces of tea, eight
ounces of fats (of which only two ounces could be taken as butter), two
ounces of jam, one ounce of cheese and one shilling's worth of meat.
Later, sweets and tinned foods of all kinds were only available 'on
points'—by giving up a specified and changing number of small green
tokens from the ration book. Bread was scarce, but unrationed during
the war; it had to be rationed from July 1946.

Yet *was* it all dull and dreary, having to 'make do'? There was,
as there always is, a great sense of satisfaction in managing to produce
edible meals from so very few ingredients, in sharing recipes, in boiling
up ends of soap tablets to make new ones, in converting and remaking
garments when clothing, fabrics and footwear were rationed in June
1941. The Ministry of Food issued special recipes and advertisements
about the properties of various foods, 'British Restaurants' provided
cheap meals in towns, and subsidized school dinners were available in
schools. Catering at home was made easier by the use of many substitute
foods—dehydrated milk and eggs, dried potato, whale meat, 'Spam'
and a curious fish called 'snoek'.

As a result of all these innovations, nobody went hungry in this
country, and many families had a more balanced diet than they had ever
had before.

The enormous improvements in housing conditions since the
war have transformed the family pattern for a great many people, and
changed the function of the kitchen. In small town houses the 'front'
room used to be used only very rarely, on special occasions, and every-

one ate and lived in the kitchen. Now, horizons have widened; with educational opportunities open to all, with television and cheap foreign travel introducing new ideas and new interests, most men, women and children not only have more space in which to live than their parents and grandparents had, but they tend to *use* that space more than before—for reading, for study, for listening to records and for hobbies as well as for watching television. Moves to new housing estates have changed many old patterns of living; the kitchen is used for cooking and perhaps for eating; the bathroom is used for laundering; and the other rooms of the house are also lived in.

The fifties and sixties were prosperous times; there was great demand for domestic goods and most kitchens became easier places to work in, with refrigerators, pressure-cookers, extractor fans, floor-polishers, washing machines, spin-dryers and dish-washers. Although a great deal still remains to be done to provide decent homes and pleasant kitchens for everyone, we know that the days when anything was considered good enough for 'below stairs' have gone for ever. Architects and designers now pay a great deal of attention to kitchen design and layout and think of the kitchen as a workshop for a skilled worker. The basement kitchen with its warren of dark passages and awkward stairs is as much a relic of a less civilized past as the scold's bridle and the ducking-stool.

Food takes as much preparing for the table as it did half a century ago, but today much of the work associated with this has been transferred from the kitchen to the factory. A revolution in the food industries has given the average housewife in the western world enormously increased leisure time. There has grown up a kind of partnership between the housewife and industry. For relatively little cost she can now buy time—that time which she would in the past have spent in scraping, washing, peeling, cutting up, sorting and mixing the food for her family.

Family life is changing in fundamental ways and many of these have particular effects upon the kitchen. There is less hard labour there, now that machinery does much of the work that hands used to do, and many women are not content to spend most of their time in the kitchen as they were when no alternatives were open to them. Moreover, most husbands are willing to help in the kitchen in ways that were not necessary when housewifery was a full-time job and when grandparents and unmarried relatives often remained part of the family circle.

As the world of the kitchen has shrunk, so has its size. Now that virtually every woman is her own cook and cleaner, washerwoman, nursemaid and gardener, economy of movement, of time, of upkeep and of running costs are studied with care. The importance of built-in cupboards, of working surfaces at a convenient height, and of the proper placing of lights, switches, handles and indicators, is now fully appreciated. The psychological effect of fresh air, sunlight and cheerful colours is accepted, too, as being as great in the kitchen as in all other parts of the house.

In past centuries, satisfactory domestic equipment was available to wealthy people, but others had to manage largely with what they could make themselves. Today, modern production can supply things of quality for everybody. Because of new materials and new opportunities, because of the housewife's growing emancipation, and because of the character of the machine itself, the best kitchen furniture and equipment is inevitably simple. Our problem is to learn to choose wisely from among the enormous variety of goods available.

A Selective Bibliography

Bayne Powell, *Housekeeping in the Eighteenth Century*
  (Murray, 1956)
Birley, *Life in Roman Britain* (Batsford, 1964)
Carson, *Colonial Virginian Cookery* (Williamsburg, 1968)
Carson, *The Polite Americans* (Macmillan, 1967)
Clark, *Prehistoric England* (Batsford, 1940)
Drummond & Wilbraham, *The Englishman's Food*
  (Cape, 1939)
Emmison, *Tudor Food and Pastimes* (Benn, 1964)
Gies, *Life in a Medieval City* (Baker, 1969)
Hartley, *Food in England* (Macdonald, 1954)
Hole, *The English Housewife in the Seventeenth Century*
  (Chatto & Windus, 1953)
James (ed.), *A Butler's Recipe Book* (CUP, 1935)
Jekyll, *Old English Household Life* (Batsford, 1925)
Kenyon, *Digging up Jericho* (Benn, 1957)
Lutes, *The Country Kitchen* (Bell, 1938)
Labarge, *A Baronial Household in the Thirteenth Century*
  (Eyre & Spottiswoode, 1965)
Mead, *The English Medieval Feast* (Allen & Unwin, 1931)
Powell, *Below Stairs* (Peter Davies, 1968)
Power, *Medieval People* (Methuen, 1924)
Scott Thompson, *Life in a Noble Household* (Cape, 1937)
Sillar, *Edinburgh's Child* (Oliver & Boyd, 1961)
Shepherd & Newton, *The Story of Bread* (Routledge, 1957)
Wright, *Clean and Decent* (Routledge, 1960)
Wright, *Home Fires Burning* (Routledge, 1964)

Index